To Rob, Simple Stories, Hope you like it!

Life Behind Bars

Stories and Encounters

CHEERS!

Kyle Branche

DEDICATION

To all the bars I've ever worked in, all the private parties and events I've ever worked at, all the bartenders, barbacks, waiters, managers, GM's and owners I've ever worked with, all the liquor reps and spirit houses, and to all the magazines, editors and publishers I've ever written for. You have been the grist for my mill for 30 years.

CONTENTS

Note: I wrote all the stories in a random mode, no chronological order of occurrence, and I've kept them that way in this book. All of the stories listed and lined up above are in the exact order in which I wrote them. Therefore, it allows the reader to pick or select at their choosing what story they prefer to read at any given time, or they can simply be read in the order here.

ACKNOWLEDGMENTS

Special thanks to bartender/friend Kellie Nicholson for her support and techs-pertise with editing and formatting on how to do this and how to do that while still keeping within an artistic vision, look and style of one's own. Much appreciated!

Special thanks to my friend Martin Veider for all things computer-related, as I would have never made it this far without your continued faith and patience with a slow-curve learner like me, and excellence in keeping my words and hard drive alive in the online world while my education never ends. I think it's time for that final upgrade!

And a last-minute thank you to photographer, Paul de Leon for catching me during a moment of prep time behind the bar up at Rancho Sol Del Pacifico out in Malibu, for the shot of me on the back cover. To see more of Paul's pic work, go to: pauldeleon.com

To view a more visual experience with the stories beyond the capabilities with words alone, there are pictures and videos that coincide with many of the stories in this book located on my Blog, where the stories originated – LABartender.wordpress.com.

Website: KylesCocktailHotel.com

1

THE EASTWOOD MOMENT

I've been bartending at the famous Gardenia Room in Hollywood for close to 22 years now, in various time capacities; full-time, part-time, on-call, etc. During this time I've also worked in a number and variety of other bars, clubs and venues throughout L.A., to the point where I can barely remember them all anymore. One week, well over 10 years ago now, the Gardenia had a four-night performance booking of Cabaret shows with Cynthia Sykes. She is the wife of producer Bud Yorkin, who's credits include the TV show "All in the Family" and the cult sci-fi movie thriller "Blade Runner."

The shows were basically packed every night with a who's who of Old Hollywood, and as a note, to this day the club has avoided the radar of the paparazzi, who would have had a field day with these shows as well as many others. The room is styled after a classic Cabaret venue, which is small, holding about 70 people. I work alone behind the bar, taking care of everyone, many a time at warp speed. There's dinner and a two-drink minimum, and the show starts at 9:00 pm. I met Bud earlier in the day, during lights and sound check, before the doors opened at 7:00 pm, when I was there to set up and prep the bar.

He handed me a selection of red wine bottles that he brought in from his cellar at home, mentioning to me to be ready during the night for when he needs one uncorked and breathing in advance, as a special guest and friend of his was to arrive at some point in time during the night. He then told me who it was. About a half hour before show time, Clint Eastwood walks in the door of the club, alone, very casual and relaxed, and easy going, as is his nature. The bar is about six feet from the door, so I pretty much notice everyone coming in, even when I'm buried with drinks.

Many celebrities young and old frequent the club on a regular basis, to the point where it's not a big deal anymore, or at least no longer intimidating. The actress Ann Rutherford (Gone with the Wind) still comes in to see shows today, and she's 90 years old. She started acting in film at the age of 15. Barbara Bain from *Mission Impossible* comes into the club as well. But when you know a little in advance that a legend and true Hollywood icon like Clint Eastwood is about to come through that door, it hits you for a moment to the point where you wish you could put seatbelts on, as it can be a touch of overwhelm.

We said hello, and as soon as I was about to gently point to Mr. Yorkin in the room, Bud noticed him at the entrance and bar, and came over to greet him. That was my signal for his fine bottle of Cabernet to be poured for two at the corner of the bar, where they stayed and chatted for quite some time. That was a good thing, as I was too busy with a full bar and waiter drinks for the floor to hang close by for long, but I kept an eye on the levels in their stemware, and always caught the right times to pour without requiring an assisted nod from either of them, though I did leave the bottle on the bar nearby, in case of self-serve emergency, or if they chose to take the bottle to their table.

The club in general draws a crowd of all ages, but at times can be predominantly older, depending on who the performer is. Therefore, I've been making not only the basic drinks and specialty cocktails behind the bar, but many classic cocktails as well throughout the whole time I've been there. Who said classic cocktails were forgotten and a thing of the past? Not here at The Gardenia!

Clint is the ultimate cool cat, just like in the movies, not interested in bringing attention to himself. Because of him, it was easy for me to remain smooth behind the bar. Bud had used a valet service for the run of shows, so when I caught a moment just before the show was starting, I went outside for a breath of fresh and to see what Clint drove to the club. The valet mentioned that he saw him park his super-charged Ford Bronco across the street in the Thrifty parking lot, and then walked across Santa Monica Blvd. on La Brea, made a left and walked over to the front door of the club.

Imagine seeing that when you're waiting in your car at the signal light, or walking alongside him for that matter. What a moment, especially when you consider that Clint knew what that area of Hollywood looked like back in the 50's and 60's, when he was shooting the show "Rawhide", not to mention the current circus variety of streetwalkers hanging around in the area today. He owned the street. He had no fear.

A small venue like this on the tight boulevard, you can blink and miss the club while driving by. This area of Santa Monica Boulevard also doubles as the original last extension of Route 66 that leads all the way to and ends at the Pacific Ocean. But for a few precious hours, Old Hollywood can let their hair down and enjoy each other's company, for the most part preferring to be called by their first names. That can take a bit of getting used to.

When you see it all happening early on, as I look over the packed room of guests at their tables dining, it's like a bunch of friends in the business gathered in a hidden living room, peach-colored and dim lit. The epitome of a club night. Norman Lear and his wife were there. Henry Mancini (who co-wrote the songs "Moon River" and "Charade" with Johnny Mercer, to name just a couple of the many) and his wife were in attendance. Chevy Chase was in. Ann Margret was in. Many more.

I picked up the phone when Raquel Welch called to say she was running a bit late and to let her friends know for her, whom she was joining. She then walks into the club about 45 minutes later, stops right at the corner of the bar and says "Hi Kyle!" The lucky seven sitting at the bar were stunned! But I won't tell you all of what she said to me over the phone before that happened, except that you knew it was her on the line. She has a distinctive voice all her own. It was very tasty . . .

The show went well. Though Cynthia wasn't the most seasoned singer, she gave it her all, which is impressive in itself in a room full of your peers. She had a great 3-piece band backing her, including pianist Paul Smith, who was Ella Fitzgerald's pianist and conductor from 1952-1978. I remember him coming to the bar and asking for a club soda to take over and sit it on an old floor speaker next to the piano. When we initially greeted and shook hands, his hand was so big that I couldn't see my hand in it. What an incredible player he was on the keys, though. Sensational tone and feel for the notes.

At the end of the show, they both came up to the same corner of the bar, and I set them up with another bottle of red and two fresh wine glasses. Once Clint knew my name, mainly by Bud calling out to me, a slight grin appeared on his face when he glanced over, likely due to the fact that his son is also named Kyle.

In the end, Clint was the last one to leave the club, hanging with us as we were cleaning up, looking at the inside corner wall calendar listing of upcoming performers next to the bar. He asked Ernie and I about the singers and who's really good. We mentioned a few to him, including Stephanie Vlahos who was popular at the time, and he nodded silently.

4

Maybe he was thinking of transforming his Hog's Breath Inn up North on the coast in Carmel to host some Cabaret of his own. A place where the song "Misty" would be a perfect fit, given his love of Jazz and the Great American Songbook, but the place would need a substantial makeover to fit the musical theme.

A few more minutes went by as he was reading some of the performer's bios, he put one of the club calendars in his coat pocket to take with him, said goodnight to us, and slowly walked out the door and into the midnight of Hollywood, maybe as he once remembered it . . .

2

THE ORIGINAL PLATINUM BLONDE

In October 2009, I bartended a private party at the old home that was once leased and lived in by actress Jean Harlow in the late 20's and early 30's, on 512 N. Palm Drive, a several block street sitting between Sunset and Wilshire. This was her last residence before she died.

It is also on record that Rita Hayworth once lived in the house, whether lease or own, I don't know. Built in 1928, the home is a lot bigger than it looks, with the 4,400 sq. ft having 5 bedrooms and 5 baths. In 2000, it sold for 2 million. In 2007 it sold for just under 4 million.

We needed two bartenders for the evening's guest count, so I called in Tami Ross, a bartending friend on the party circuit, to work alongside.

It was my second or third time working a party there. I was able to take a picture of the bar in the house in its original condition, as we were prepping up from about 5:00 pm to open it at 7:00 pm for about 100-150 guests. To think of the cocktail parties they had at the home way back in the day! In the backyard is a lighted tennis court and plenty of room to relax and enjoy the afternoon, or evening! I wondered if they ever made Mojitos as much as we made that night, as well as many other drinks of choice, along with a selection of wines red and white, and a few different beers.

One can imagine Clark Gable making drinks behind the bar, as Harlow and Gable, who called her "Sis", were best friends. William Powell, Walter Huston, Louis B Mayer as well as many other possibilities. Unfortunately, Jean died in 1937 at the young age of only 26, from a uremic poisoning brought on by acute nephritis.

Jean's real name was Harlean Carpenter. Born in Kansas City on March 3, 1911. Last year marked the 100 year anniversary of her birthday, had she been alive today. She was also the godmother of Millicent Siegel, daughter of the notorious mobster Benjamin "Bugsy" Siegel. She had two famous superstitions: She always wore a lucky ankle chain on her left leg. Back then she had to be one of the first wearing an anklet. Her other is a lucky mirror in her dressing room. She wouldn't leave the room without first looking in it.

Across the street from her lived Lee Duncan, who was the owner of the famous canine superstar, Rin Tin Tin. As the story goes, when the dog passed away at the age of 16, Harlow went over to the house and cradled the dog's head in her lap.

Setting up the bar was always a bit of a task depending on if you're using real glassware, as there's basically no true backbar, and the underbar still has the original stainless steel in place. Therefore, *mise-en-place* always had to be as efficient as possible, though the wine rack built in the wall in back helped a little.

All the archways throughout the home remained the same, so pretty much the entire property inside and out was kept to its' original style and architectural design. Fitting, given the history. Though a multi-storied home, I've yet to get the chance to peruse upstairs. Maybe next time. Due to security being out in front of the home before the guests arrived, I didn't get a shot of the front, but it's beautifully laid out with a veranda and fine tile up to the front door, and a waterfall in the open flat part of the yard.

When I was outside next to the truck putting my dress shirt on for the gig, I took a shot of the front of another house before the sunset, just two doors down at 508, that used to be owned in the 50's by Marilyn Monroe and Joe DiMaggio, shortly after they were married. Marilyn idolized Harlow, as Jean was "The Original Platinum Blonde".

The party went well for the most part. There's always some imperfections that occur during the night, where the two of us side-by-side behind this bar makes for quite the compact movement, or somewhere else in the house where guests are hanging out and enjoying themselves, shuffling in the bar area, stepping out to the back patio, and appetizer tray-passers who have to weave in and out of the constantly moving floor.

I had Tami leave a little earlier after the bar slowed down later in the night, about an hour before I cleaned up the bar. Putting my sizeable bar kit back together, I closed up the bar except for an area of self-serve I set-up on the bar top for the remaining friends of the family, got paid, said my goodbyes and slowly walked out the front door. Sticking around long enough behind the bar alone, I was hoping for the possibility of an otherworldly visitation or two, just in case they wanted to make an appearance. I'm "open" as they say, to be their path of least resistance. No such luck this time around!

The weather had changed in the previous hours of the bars' peak volume period, as it was raining a light mist with plenty of new cloud coverage above. The temperature was perfect and slightly balmy on the skin. Maybe it had to do a little bit with a mixture of the night's perspiration on my face and arms.

The streets of Beverly Hills are wide for the most part, and very clean with tall palms. It's not everyday you get to hang out and relax in an area like this, much less in the middle of the night, and the gorgeous slow rain that L.A. is always in need of, gently lit up from the occasional street light in the short distance.

My work is done for the evening. I can slow my mental gears down, shove my bar kit in the passenger seat of the truck, hang my collared shirt back up, light a smoke and go stand in the middle of the dark, empty street of the famous Palm Drive for a while, arms stretched out and up towards the sky, breathing in all the history of what once was, before I take the road home back over the hill and into the West San Fernando Valley.

In honor of Ms. Harlow, I'll leave you with two of her quotes:

"I was not a born actress. No one knows it better than I. If I had any latent talent, I have had to work hard, listen carefully, do things over and over and then over again in order to bring it out."

"Men like me because I don't wear a brassiere. Women like me because I don't look like a girl who would steal a husband. At least not for long."

3

CHRISTMAS EVE
ON MULHOLLAND DRIVE

It's another December 24ᵗʰ, and once again, I know where I'm scheduled to be tonight. People are heading home from their shortened work days and maybe some office parties, possibly making a last-minute mall stop, and I'm slowly getting ready to go to work for the evening. No matter where bartenders work for the most part, it's rare to have a holiday off. But when you work private like I do, the "eves" are basically the same thing. It's that time of the year when it gets darker earlier, so I need to clear my table of any miscellany-to-do's sooner than normal, so it seems.

I trek out on my mountain bike to take my Netflix DVD over to Lois and Kathleen at Mail Box Etc. and to drop a biscuit off for Shana the dog, go to the quick store to grab some nuts for the backyard squirrel posse, pick-up a couple pieces from the dry cleaners, and as I roll back through the residential, I stop by the open garage where a neighborhood friend of mine, Mark Knight, lives with his family, and we catch up for a few minutes, as he lives just 10 houses down from me. He was the founder and lead guitarist for the 90's band Bang Tango. He still jams today with his band Worry Beads and fronts his own band Mark Knight and the

Unsung Heroes, along with teaching guitar in his garage studio. Mark is also an excellent wood craftsman.

I love this area of the valley, Woodland Hills, having lived here for some 17 years now. I'm on my bike more than in my truck, doing errands and what not. I get back to the house with my things in tow, retrieve my bar gear from the garage and into the truck, shower and dress with a quick-shave electric, and I'm off.

Luckily, the 101 freeway corridor at this time isn't hell's pit stop, so I'm cruising East into the deeper fray of L.A., exit off Laurel Canyon and head South to Ventura Boulevard for a quick bite at Good Earth restaurant. Driving up into the hills, I find myself third-gearing it up the winding incline. As I'm passing by, the house off the side of the road was still there from over a year ago that during heavy rains, it broke from its foundation and slid down a length of canyon wall and stopped about twenty feet in front of the main road, in tact !

Reaching Mulholland Drive, I make a left moving East a little more until I slip into the old, quieter part of the long road, closest into the Hollywood Hills. It's dark when I arrive, and speaking of cliff houses, I'm about to enter into one, an older build from back in time and space. For the last six years or more, I've been the requested bartender for the legendary celebrity public relations maestro of the media, Dale Olsen, for his long-running Christmas Eve party of old friends, business associates, directors, producers, writers, composers, actors, musicians and radio personalities.

Chris Stone usually works with me on this gig, as he takes the kitchen duties while I've got the bar, opposite ends of the house. Chris is a good guy to work with, but I haven't seen him in a while. His work shifted a bit. First and foremost, he's an actor and stand-in, but his brother operates a home security company. Last time I spoke with him on the phone, he was handling heavy hours working security detail on the graveyard shift up at Jennifer

Aniston's house. I let him know I was pushing to bartend one of her parties !

Helping out Dale and his partner Eugene with their party is always a lot of fun, yet never lacking challenge to keep up with. The home is like walking into a cozy museum. The bar is this tiny, but at least bar-height, service bar area. Though space was limited, it was still workable, had a sink to the side, and a framed invitation to the White House on the wall. There's also the old, lighted Olympia beer frame, still working with its waterfall. I'm thinking late 60's, early 70's. To the right of the bar is an incredible collection of vinyl (LP's), perfectly shelved and tight from the floor to the ceiling.

Dale's close to 80 now, so you can imagine the history in the house. His client list from the past to his semi-retired present is impressive to say the least. One quick note that Eugene mentioned to me about his past is in the first week of June, 1968, he had breakfast with Bobby Kennedy at the Ambassador Hotel on the morning of the late night that Bobby was assassinated by Sirhan Sirhan.

One small side note about the hotel is, the lighting guy for many of the shows at The Gardenia Room, Matt Haimsohn, his mother worked in the offices of the Ambassador for many years. He told me that when he was a kid, and this was probably in the 60's, he used to hang out at the hotel with his mother, but would easily wander off for periods of time. There were small cottages on the property, and the waiters showed Matt the entrance to the secret tunnels that were used as room service for the special bungalows reserved for the rich and famous.

I told them both about a DVD I have of a documentary titled "Off the Menu" – The Last Days of Chasen's, that was produced right before they closed their doors in April 1995. I'm watching it at home, the camera pans to a table, and there's Dale sitting in a booth with Rod Steiger, getting ready to order dinner.

I remember bartending at the house in the Summer during a new book release party of Shirley MacLaine's "The Camino", of which I happily received a signed copy of. I'm making drinks for a while in rhythm with the arrival of the guests, and I hear this voice from about four feet in back of me. I turned around and it was Elliot Gould asking me for a diet coke. This is just how it goes for us hired hands !

Dale and Eugene have mentioned to Chris and I before, saying "You guys should have been here in the 80's when we were hosting parties all the time." This night before Christmas Day they've held annually for probably a couple decades or more, is made up of all males, no females. I don't know the preferred reason why. I think it's more of just a ritual for the boys at this point, you know, like Hollywood skull and bones but without the robes and candelabra! And these guys are old school, so they can drink.

Though many, there's a couple interesting notables who show up, including Earl Holliman who starred in Police Woman with Angie Dickinson, and was in one of my favorite films from the 80's, Sharkey's Machine. The poet and singer Rod McKuen was there as well. It's great to catch up with them each year at the bar, and they're interested in what I have going on too, which is cool. Knowing Chris and I were probably two of the few token straight guys at the party, we felt untouchable! They were really a great bunch of guys and it was a pleasure to serve them.

Both Dale and Eugene put the time and effort in as executive chefs instead of hiring a caterer. This makes Chris' job of the final cook, prep, and serve a little easier, and he knows how the boys want it buffet-placed on the dinner table so everyone can serve themselves. Eugene was a singer and dancer. He's very joyous and happy this time of year, with a great sense of humor, and a powerful baritone voice remarkable just to listen to when he speaks. He tells us stories of when he was a performer back in the day. Amazing stuff !

Dale has wrapped Christmas gifts that he fetches from underneath the tree and passes out to each of his guests after dinner and just before dessert and coffee. A yearly ritual as well, and a very cool one at that.

When initially walking into the home, you're on the top floor where the bar, living areas and kitchen are, and the deck outside overlooks the canyon, as well as the Pacific Ocean and Catalina Island on a clear day. The lower floor has the sleeping quarters and the like, and the pool right outside. A little reverse of the norm, except for the pool.

Chris and I do a final clean to our work stations, getting all the glassware dry and back in the bar cabinet. The four of us chat about the night for a few minutes. I even see Dale and Eugene when they come into the Gardenia on occasion to see a show, like the Tyne Daly performances from over a year ago. We say our goodbyes and hug each other before we head out the door and gate. You miss them, and pray that you'll see them once again.

It's a little chill outside, but not cold due to overcast. The marine layer is moving in like fast-forward footage, so close on the top of Mulholland you feel like you can almost touch it. Our vehicles are a short walking distance away from each other, so Chris and I chat about things for a few minutes. Then, as he expected, and as he's done before. I asked him to lead us in a prayer as we stood in one of the lanes of the road – of thanks and health, for the evening, for the boys, for our lives, and for the night ride home.

It was after midnight, early Christmas morning . . .

4

THE DUCATI EVENT

In the Summer of 2011 I bartended a party for the unveiling of a new Ducati motorcycle in conjunction with Lorenzo Cycles. Their shop is on La Cienega in L.A., and this is where the event took place. I was working with Bill and Emily of Conquest Entertainment, who work with John Paul DeJoria of Patron tequila in producing all of their brand-sponsored bar events here in town, as well as other things. I've worked many of their events over the last four years, and it's always a pleasure to be behind the bar for them.

However, for this party, Emily was out of town on vacation, so she set me up with all the detail information by email in advance, and I worked with Bill the rest of the way on featured drink recipes and what fresh juices I needed to pick up at the store nearby the house, along with glassware and a few bags of ice to start out with, as I was told the shop was going to have more ice delivered or picked up. Patron was renting my custom portable bar with black linens, so I loaded that in the back of my Ranger STX around noon that day. It's good to have a truck in Los Angeles!

I also had to be in contact with Joel, the manager of the cycle shop, and Chad Guerlich, who represents Lorenzo Cycles and the owner, actor Lorenzo Lamas. There was a bonus feature added to the event. Chad emailed me some release forms to sign and fax back to the producer of the show "Private Chefs of Beverly Hills", as that night they were shooting the first episode of their second season, in the party.

The office for Conquest is in Santa Monica, just a couple blocks away from the beautiful area around Montana Ave. After grabbing everything at the store, I headed out on the road at 1:00 pm, taking Topanga Canyon through the mountains, which about 12 miles later lands you right on Pacific Coast Highway. Cruising East for a few miles along the water's edge, I made a left and went up what's known as the California Incline, taking you to the top of the cliff and into Santa Monica.

Conveniently, my favorite Mexican restaurant, Casa Escobar, is close by, so I drive a couple miles up on Wilshire for a bite to eat, to help keep my power up for the long day/night ahead, as I never count on anything available to eat on location, even with knowing the show was going to be tray-passing appetizers. I try to avoid digesting mouths of food while I'm working. I like a clean palate when I'm on the job. But if I get hungry . . .

The office is just a mile away, so I trek over and meet up with Bill. We chat for a minute about the event and he shows me the boxes of spirits product to load up and take with me, and brand merchandise (mats, shakers, garnish tray, napkin holder, fruit squeezers, shirts etc) to have placed on the bar top. I hand him a copy of my new drink book "Cocktails of the American West", which he was pleased to receive, then I began carrying things out to the truck. He said he might show up later on, and that J.P. would be there too.

Instead of taking the freeway again, I trekked down Olympic Boulevard all the way into La Cienega and the heart of L.A., arriving in the small parking area behind the shop and through the alley close to 4:00 pm. The Food Channel show crew were already there setting up audio, video, lights, and food! I met Joel and the owner of the Ducati shop, and we took a quick walk around the interior of the store to decide on the best placement of the bar. Having quite a bit to unload, I got started as soon as possible, as the carry back and forth can eat up some time in a hurry.

The setting up and prepping went fine, pretty much had what I needed, and pitcherized the three featured drinks so I can shake and pour at a fast pace. I had six bottles of Patron Silver for the night, some Citronge, and a bottle of Pyrat rum to the visible side. It's always nice to have close to an hour after the bar is ready and before showtime so I can gather and refresh myself.

I go out to the truck and change into my all-black clothing attire (with Patron shirt) for the bar, have a smoke while bullshitting in the back parking lot with some of the show's grip and tech guys, eventually meeting the producers of the show, and to get the previous physical laboring off my mind and into a ready-to-go mode of greeting, serving, chatting and making drinks until the end. I didn't have an assistant with me, so I was working the entire gig solo and self-contained from start to finish. The ultimate front-line representative.

I walked into the bar a few minutes before it actually opened so I can final adjust anything mise-en-place. There were many people moving around doing many things in the general area of the bar, getting ready for the production of the combination event and episode taping. They brought in a DJ who was set up about six feet behind me to the left and up two steps. The staff of the shop had to clear away some apparel racks and a few of the currently sold motorcycles, moving them closer to the walls. When you're in the shop for this period of time, the scent of leather and rubber start to permeate.

I opened the bar a little before 7:00 pm, mainly just to get my engine going. The guests hadn't started arriving yet, but there were a few people around who were thirsty. I also had a small, clear, hard-plastic bucket to the side full of ice and mini-waters for anyone to grab on their own. Chad had arrived. We introduced ourselves and talked about how the night was going to go. I'm never nervous in these types of settings, no matter how potentially chaotic they can be. I've worked so many of them. It's easier once you know what the lowdown is, and being the man behind the bar doesn't hurt either. It's a comfortable cage barrier where people fear to tread!

Yet, I was wondering when their ice delivery was going to happen, as someone in charge didn't quite take the timing of that all important bar necessity to the degree that I have to in my position, which is why I prefer to just bring it all myself, but the meltage factor comes into play during a hot day sitting and riding in back of the truck for whatever amount of time. There's many things to watch out for, but ice, glassware and product are the lifeblood of a bar, and should never be late or insufficient for the needs at hand. It eventually arrived. Mind relieved. I'm glad we didn't have an ice bar for this event, as Patron has provided many times in the past and present.

Lorenzo arrived with his "OMG" fiancee, and I promptly served up the first batch of drinks to them and Brad, as the four of us chatted at the bar. Then the guys asked me when J.P. was showing up, and I mentioned he was supposed to arrive around 9:00 pm. At that time, someone had wheeled in the custom Patron Harley-Davidson that was sitting in back earlier, for J.P. to see for the first time. Pretty awesome bike. Wish I would have had my camera with me, but I thought Bill was going to have a photographer there as usual, but they didn't this time. Didn't learn of that until after I left the house. There was a photographer hired by Chad though, a guy by the name of Damian Rinaldi (.com) to take care of their end, and they would probably send some over to Bill later on anyway.

Proceedings slowly got under way, and I found myself once again in the rhythm and groove of the night. In total there were probably

60 people. Fine with me. The easier the better sometimes, but it can get rockin' with drinks, of which it did. On the fly I created another drink, the "Triple Threat", simply by mixing all three drink flavors together. It was quite a hit! I have six different shakers for use in my bar kit, so four of them ended up getting consistent play. Camera guys were all around the bar catching some close-up B-roll of me shakin', slingin' and juicin', so hopefully some of it sticks in the episode. It was interesting to watch as they shot with the show's stars "live" in the room, and moved about during the evening until they completed.

Racing legend, Larry Pegram, was there making a special appearance, and when J.P. showed up is when they had everyone together to start the announcements and introductions. All went well for the night's festivities, and six more bottles of Silver gone like water. With my work for another one-off event like this, there's always the beginning, the middle and the end. Produced like any other show for the most part, and the goal is always to pull it off. I love making drinks for people, and that's what keeps me cruising to the end.

All involved start to break everything down, including me with the bar and full side kit of floor mats, ice tubs, trash tubs, product, linens, shakers, and on and on. You get to witness the dragging part of the night, when our energies go from high to low. The finish line feels good of a job well done, which certainly helps the mind during clean-up, packing, dumping and re-loading time. The producer's assistant introduced herself to me at the bar just before taping started. She was really cute and petite, so I remembered to give her one of the Patron sleeveless black t-shirts in girl's sizes that I had with me, packed in a box. Happy girl !

5

Secret Serviced

In early January 2008, I got a call from a staffing agency I'm connected with to work a special event, of a political nature. The Reagan Library is located off the Olsen Road exit on the 23 freeway in Simi Valley, about 30 minutes from where I live, going West.

Over the phone, Tim asked me if I was available to work on Wednesday, January 30. I said "Yes, I'm open in my gig calendar". He replied "Good, you'll be working a long lunch day and dinner night bartending in the private quarters upstairs over at the The Reagan on the day and during the evening of the Republican National Debate", held down below near Air Force One.

Tim mentioned "The Secret Service needs to do a full background check on you, so I'll need copies of your current driver's license, social security card, and passport faxed to me as soon as you can, so I can forward it onto them. "Are you okay with all this ?" "Sure" I said, throwing all caution to the wind. Out of curiosity, I wanted to see what the result would be, pass or fail. After all, I'm no angel!

A week later, I received clearance and booked the gig in for solid. I'd worked previous events at the library before through an in-house caterer, Command Performance, so I knew what I was walking into, but the private quarters would be a first. On the day, I drove up sometime before noon. All of us had to pull our vehicles into the park across the street from the library, on Olsen Road. A security van of substantial size was centered near the main parking areas, and we had to walk over, show our ID, and get our security badges.

From that point, and due to parking and top security limitations, we were shuttled up the hill. While waiting a while for the next one to come around, I went back to the truck and quickly burned one to calm the nerves, then gathered my reduced bar kit and required bar shirt and tie, as I already had my black slacks and work shoes on. Throwing a half-stick of spearmint gum in my mouth, I was ready to roll.

It was a beautiful day outside. Too bad I was going to be inside to not enjoy it! But there were more pressing matters at hand, like the future fate of the country, with nothing less than a big group of GOP lifers who can't seem to grow a worthy candidate for president that even they like. What they didn't know, is that just a month previous, in December 2007, I was asked to work solo behind the main bar for about 75 people of prominence in a private home in Beverly Hills, just a mile or so off the 405 freeway and Sunset Boulevard for a Democratic Jewish Fundraiser for none other than the candidate and speaker of the night, Hillary Clinton. I'll get into this side of the aisle in more detail on another post.

Matt was a regular bartender there at the time that I had worked with before and eventually on a few of my larger private Persian gigs in Beverly Hills, so he showed me around upstairs and we both started setting up the bars. It's always nice to know someone you'll be pouring drinks with.

It's one of those long days where there are various down-times between levels of activity throughout the library and the open bars. If you've never been there before, it's quite an impressive facility to visit when you get the chance. All kinds of displays and memorabilia, this one particularly bent in the direction of a country and western lifestyle mixed with a healthy dose of Hollywood and film. The collection of President Reagan's belt buckles alone would take some minutes to steer your eyes away from and move onto some other area of interest, not to mention the opportunity to walk in and through Air Force One.

After the upstairs lunch crowd was through and gone, and watching from big windows in the distance above as the floor down below continued it's strict and formal set-up of chairs and tables and what not for the night's festivities, I went and had a little bite to eat with some of the staff I was working with. Soon after, I walked outside to roam around and get some fresh air for a few minutes, as my VIP badge credentials allow, and to observe what everyone else was doing. As one can imagine, there are cameras all over the place, inside and outside the entire property.

Going back upstairs to the private quarters, it was quite empty as expected. Right there in the middle of rooms and corridors, the offices of both Ronald and Nancy Reagan were open and next to each other, as how it should be. At that moment, I'm thinking to myself, damn, I forgot to bring my digital camera!

However, I did have my cell phone with me. As I walked into their warm and comfortable office spaces, decorated and clean, moving slowly from hers to his, hovering just inches away from the President's desk, I gave my mother a call in Arizona. With my parents being long-time Republicans, they were thrilled to hear where I was calling from. I kept her on the phone for a spell, letting her know what the office was filled with, including the picture on his desk together with four other Presidents.

I then heard someone coming down the hall from a ways away, so I said goodbye to my mother and walked out the other side door towards the back of the office and into the main living room, and acted like I had been standing there for some time. I didn't care if security could see me through the camera, at least they knew the truth. It was the suspicion from others I wanted to avoid. Conveniently in sight, looking out the picture window and slightly down the rolling hill at the rear of the building, is the area of ground where the President is laid to rest. Simi Valley is a beautiful place, and along with his ranch high up in the Santa Barbara area, were two of his favorite spots on earth.

I started setting up a third station for champagne service about fifteen feet away from the main elevator that close to 150 guests would be coming out of shortly after the debate was finished. I didn't know what bar I'd be working out of at that time, and it really didn't matter all that much anyway. Sometimes, if you just let things happen, surrendering controls, you'll end up in the right spot.

As it got underway, we watched for a while on the TV monitors built-in near the ceiling, with a sense of isolation from the moment-by-moment tired punches and jabs reflective of the unnecessarily long campaign trails. It almost became a match of the last man standing. I'd be dust in the wind too if I had to go through such an endless ordeal. Who wouldn't? I mean, how can you even get a good night's sleep in the middle of all of that on your mind? And you're supposed to run a country? That's right! You will run it, right into the ground!! The structure of these institutions needs to be changed.

I walked over to the far end of the room where, looking down below, the long blocked-off staircase seemed to go around at least a half-circle, with a security guard detailed at the front. Off the top edge was a huge, black grand piano, that of the concert stage size. I went over to it with the shy internal thought of sitting down and seeing if it was in tune enough to tickle the ivories in the most silent way for a while. Though tempting, I held off so as not to raise the hairs under any hats, and out of respect for those who asked me in. There was an 8 x 10 frame on the top saying this piano was donated to the Reagan Library by American pianist and composer, John Williams. Enough said! I would have loved to hear the sound of it though, I have to admit.

The debate concluded. It was over.

At our bar stations, we had the basic well and call cocktails, beer, wine, and had poured crisp, cold champagne in advance so the guests could just pick up and graze if preferred, while the appetizers began to pass. It soon filled up with the usual suspects, dignitaries, formers and the like, and then John McCain eventually paced out of the elevator, in perfect vision just steps away from me, basically with his head down, as though he was about to get the tongue-lashing of his life for wrecking his parent's car.

Who knows where he disappeared to, but he wasn't around for long. He probably went to speak to Nancy Reagan for a minute, who was sitting down in the couch in the living room, with her interior decorator next to her, getting ready to watch the televised documentary of her husband and family.

I feel for the man. Not only has he been through enough for one lifetime, he's put himself through even more. I wish I could hug him, and say "Mr. McCain, we all love you for your dedicated service to your/our country. Now could you please, for all of our concerns, retire for your own health and well-being and enjoy some golf and leisure. We think you've earned it."

I tell you, when you're around the air of these people for hours like I was, and that I've been in the past with other events, you gather the slow perception that all of them have a true and deep addiction to politics, like crack bad! This is not something they give up easily. There will be a fight before they drop to the canvas, regardless of their age. It is a career of buying favors and influence along the way to hold on to your post, difficult to say goodbye to. Talk about a cancer on top of a bad habit. There was even the energetic stench of a few lobbyists cruising like hungry coyotes even after devouring a plate of food in mere seconds.

Governor Schwarzenegger was supposed to show up using the utility/service elevator, but failed to appear, more than likely embarrassed by the lame exchange, whispering to Mrs. Reagan still sitting down, that it was the most boring debate he had ever seen, as the word trickled upstairs light speed. The other candidates were no-shows as well, as far as I could tell.

Deliberately, I left the bar with a full bottle of red and two fresh, clean stems so I could roam, pour, greet and schmooze a little, just for fun, and to avoid being stoic behind the wood for too long. Not a night for that ! Upon that walk, I noticed past Governor Pete Wilson (91'-99') was empty of drink, so I kindly approached him and asked if he would like a glass of wine, as he was about to sit down at a table with others. He responded with great appreciation. I can really put it (the charm) on when I need or want to.

The documentary lasted for quite some time, and Mrs. Reagan, instantly providing the strongest presence and grace on the entire floor, sat and watched it from start to finish. I was in and out of the living room many times during the dinner, observing the pleasantry of people surrounding her. She could outlast all of us.

The night began to fade, and it was time to cleanup. Finally, an 11-hour shift on my feet comes to a close. Nights like these make me happy that I wear three layered pairs of socks. Saying goodbye and thanks to our wonderful floor manager, Kim, and the rest of the staff, I headed outside to where the shuttle arrives, to take us back down to the park.

Strangely enough, with everyone fatigued on the bus, sitting next to me was Steve Lentz, the reporter for KFWB News 980, located on Wilshire in L.A.. We started chatting, and he asked me what I do. I told him I was a private bartender, and he responded as though he'd never heard of such a thing before. I smiled and laughed inside. He thought for a moment and said with almost a suitcase of camera and sound gear in his lap, "I'll bet you have some intriguing stories to tell about your experiences with everywhere you're hired?". I said "Yes, as a matter of fact, I do".

He gave me his card, and mentioned to call or email him to possibly set up a time to come down to the station for a live interview. I said "Sure, I'd love to. Thanks. I'll be in touch". I did just that. I sent this story to him, to see if he's still interested in keeping his word after a couple years, only to find out that he had moved on from the station.

6

THERE ARE NO SMALL ROLES

The years of 85'-87', I was bartending at Stuart Anderson's Black Angus Restaurant in Burbank, California. It sat right off the 5 Freeway, between Bombay Bicycle Club and Bobby McGee's. Still a young bartender then, I was fortunate enough to work with some high-volume guys that brought me up to speed. All of them had been there for some years already, and I was a transfer from a new Embassy Suites Hotel in Phoenix, Arizona, as at that time, both were owned by the Marriot Corporation.

I made the move not only because of the convenience that my father was working for Lockheed Aircraft in Burbank, though lived down the road in Sylmar at the time, but that I wanted to enroll in acting class in Hollywood. So I had a job and a roof over my head to make a fresh, new start. But it wasn't easy. I was a bit young and wild with energy, and just needed a space to gather myself, get solid, do good work, get used to the roads so I wouldn't get lost on every turn, and find an acting teacher.

Matt, Chris, and Ronnie certainly put me through my paces behind the bar, with Barry the manager watching me to make sure everything was alright. I was young and he knew it, so I definitely needed the extra training, coming from a new hotel in Phoenix that was still ironing out its wrinkles when I left only after seven months due to unfairly being passed over for a promotion because the other barback/bartender's girlfriend was a cocktail waitress there. However, driving to California in the middle of the night in my 74' Fiat sports car with $85 in my pocket, leaving the girl I was staying with behind, it was a blessing in disguise.

This was back when the Angus was promoting the nightclub end of their bars, and out of 115 in the chain at that time, we were always running #1 and #2 in overall sales with the Angus in Anchorage, Alaska, believe it or not. This was a popular area for clubbing in the 80's, aside from Hollywood and Sunset, with a mixture of locals, college crowd, and some celebs, as we were just down the road from the studios on Olive Avenue. With the three bars right next to each other, it was also comically known as the "Herpes Triangle", with the Holiday Inn Tower just walking distance across the street.

The waiters at Bobby McGee's dressed up in their own themed uniforms, and at that time, Kato Kaelin was a waiter/actor there, disguised as a baseball player, and his ex-wife, Cindy, was a waiter/floor manager over at Bombay. So all of us partied at each other's bars on certain nights off, like a bar crawl without the need to get in a car. The last time I saw Kato was in 1992, when he showed up at a club in Santa Monica where I was bartending, called Denim & Diamonds. He showed up in the late afternoon when I was setting up the main bar for the night, as he had got the okay from the managers to come in and shoot the introduction for a new pilot show. We hadn't seen heads or tails of each other for some years, so we just laughed and caught up a little bit.

I lived with my father and his wife in a clean, upscale mobile home park (yes, it was a double-wide!), but the park had an excellent recreation room, pool and Jacuzzi, and it was an older crowd, which was pleasant for the peace of mind I needed for new thoughts and directions. On my days off, I would go and read and relax in the Rec. room, play pool, and take a swim. I eventually met the manager of the park one day, as he was retired there with his wife. We got to talking about some goals I had, and I mentioned that I wanted to get into an acting class. In an unexpected moment of happenstance, he told me that his son is a quite well-known International acting teacher by the name of Dominic DeFazio. I couldn't believe how this felt so meant-to-be.

Dominic was not only teaching in L.A., but for a long period of time, he was also one of Lee Strasberg's teachers in New York. Needless to say, I was soon in touch with him, and we set up a time to meet. I had never been on stage before, but felt it in my guts, so I needed to explore this opportunity. He mentioned to me that I needed to first audition, and on stage at his rented studio space in Hollywood, just off of Cahuenga Boulevard, in front of his entire current class. I picked a scene from "All the President's Men", where I played Robert Redford's character, in the office of the Washington Post as he received the call from "Deep Throat" transferred to his desk.

Shaking with a bit of sweat, I made it through the entire scene. He was quiet for some moments, with his hand going back and forth over his forehead, sitting in the front row of the seated theatre. I didn't know what to think, as the entire class was still and stoic as well. As I stood there feeling naked to the core, he asked " You've never acted or been on stage before?". I said "No, this is my first time". He took a deep breath and started to evaluate the performance of the scene. It turned out to be surprisingly positive, more than I expected, and ending with the line "I can't believe you've never acted before". I passed the audition!

It was a great class and a wonderful experience. I was in for about two years, but there were times where he would go to Italy and teach for four weeks at a stretch, so we all got a respite.

I played in several scenes in class with others, which was really enjoyable. One actor I did a scene with happened to be Charles Bukowski's wife, Linda Lee. He picked her up a couple times from class as we were all standing outside on the street, so I was fortunate to be introduced to him by Linda as her acting partner, as we had talked a couple times over the phone, but he chatted with Dominic mostly. I was a bit new to his work at the time. I was only 26 then, but looked like I was about 15.

Within this time, I read and was cast in the young son part of "The Pawnbroker" for a possible run at the Odyssey Theatre in Santa Monica, but for some reasons unknown to me, it ended up not getting staged. Funding, more than likely.

Ronnie, my bartending co-pilot at the Angus, was also an actor, and an ex-Cuban boxer. He was big and strong, but very nice. He knew what I was trying to achieve, and though I was young, he asked me if I would be interested in reading for a small part that an old playwright friend of his had written, called "Cherry Blossom Lane". I said "Sure, I'd love to". I hadn't seen it, but it didn't matter to me. I needed the experience. There were three older ladies in the play, as well as a daughter, and me.

We initially met for a table reading at an old, classic home in Hollywood, owned by one of the older female actors. Well, that lady happened to be the famous character actress, Ann Doran. With a long history of roles in both film and television spanning over decades, she also played the role of James Dean's mother in "Rebel Without a Cause". The father role was played by the actor Jim Backus, who played Thurston Howell III in the television show "Gilligan's Island". There were many great and new, young actors of the time in it as well, including Natalie Wood, Sal Mineo, and even Dennis Hopper, who happened to be the only actor that was in all three of James Dean's movies, "Giant" and "East of Eden" being the other two.

But I didn't know until after the first reading, when Ronnie came up and told me after a break. He needed to be thanked for that! The last thing I needed was to be intimidated by a legend. But I was such a young, naïve novice, that it probably wouldn't have mattered all that much anyway. At the end of the reading for the day, and a half-empty glass of ice tea in my hand, I slowly walked over to her in the living room. She was so nice and pleasant, and as I almost felt out of place, I couldn't help but to ask her what James Dean was like, so I did, but as sweet as I could.

She said "Well, James was a nice kid, but with a lot of pent-up energy, and I was like a second mother to him while he was here in Hollywood. He would sometimes come here to the house fairly late at night, a little drunk or high or both, and we would talk for some time either here in the living room or out on the porch if it was nice out, as he always had a lot of questions, and he would chat away. Then after quite a while, he would take off and go home".

We eventually did a reading on stage a couple weeks later at the Long Beach Playhouse, but it never took off so we could make a run of it, unfortunately.

Ann Doran passed away in 2000 at the age of 89. Her mother, Rose Allen, was also an actress. She passed away in 1977 at the age of 92.

I love Old Hollywood. That's why I still love working at The Gardenia Room. They still come in.

There are no small roles . . . . .

7

JUST ANOTHER DAY AT LAKESIDE, EXCEPT FOR #12

I worked behind the bars at the famous Lakeside Golf Club from 1999-2002. Nestled away and off the beaten path, it sits over the city borderlines of the Burbank/Toluca Lake area of the San Fernando Valley, yet literally just a golf swing from the Warner Brothers and Burbank Studios across Olive Avenue, with NBC and Walt Disney Studios nearby, and the Smokehouse restaurant just up the street from the gated security entrance to the club property.

Lakeside is a private golf club, not open to the general public and surrounding community, like a country club would be. It has an amazing history, and the hundreds of members pay a hefty price for membership and exclusivity, even though a couple years before I started working there they were offered $1 Billion for it by a private Japanese business group. It was turned down.

From high up in the back lot of Universal Studios, looking down and Eastward, it basically overlooks the club course and property. Lakeside may have never happened if it wasn't for the fact that in the 1920's, the Wilshire Golf Club wouldn't allow celebrities, entertainers and professional athletes to become members.

In 1924, a group of a dozen Hollywood businessmen met in a boardroom at the Hollywood Athletic Club on Sunset Boulevard and worked out a deal for the piece of property in the valley's Westside that was a huge expanse of orchards at the time. Lakeside was officially formed on May 12 of that same year. With Scotsman Max Behr being selected as the course designer, Lakeside officially opened on November 14, 1925.

During my second year there, the club celebrated it's 75th anniversary with a book of its history. The production of the book itself was limited to be distributed to its membership only. I never got my hands on one except for a minute when I was allowed to glance through it on the desk of the General Manager's office. However, I did get a typed 3-page copy of the foreword that was written by Bob Hope, and still have it today. The tail end is in his own handwriting, and says "Lakeside, thanks for the memories."

They also produced a 50-year anniversary book in 1975, written by Norm Blackburn, with only 1,150 copies made as another in-house limited edition. Out of curiosity, I went to the online site AbeBooks.com, and there was one copy of each available. The 50-year at $500, and the 75-year at $460.

Loaded with a history of famous members and professional people of power, past and present, it's a place where these alpha males can kick back, relax like a home away from home, and have fun with their pals. A mixture of individuals who've earned it, who deserve it, who married into it, and those who just got plain lucky!

On the walls of the main bar and clubhouse hang headshots by the hundreds, original frames that have been there for decades. It was always a treat for me to figure out who this and that person was, as I'm pretty good at knowing so many, but I admit Lakeside stumped the hell out of me for a while, yet it was easy enough just to ask an older member of the club, as they know everyone.

Actors, writers, producers, directors, agents, managers, lawyers, doctors, dentists, the chairman of Arco Petroleum, and a host of others were members. Whoever could afford it, but you had to be invited in from another current member and a vote was taken. Even the 94-year old grand-daughter of the man who founded the Mormon church in Utah was one of the oldest members. How's that for interesting fellowship in a soup of high society?

During late afternoons, she would be sitting quietly at a table out in the terrace lounge by herself with some ice tea or lemonade in front of her, gazing out at the day. In the distance and direction of her vision is the actual Lake Toluca, which could only be seen from inside the club property. A home across the lake is where W.C. Fields once lived. It was said that in the early morning hours you could watch him from the club as he chased ducks off his lawn back into the water.

There was a fine piano in the corner of the lounge, and occasionally I would hit a break time where I'd be able to go over, sit down and play five or ten minutes for her, some slow improv melody fitting the sound and memories of days gone by. She was always so appreciative of it, though she didn't need to thank me, as it was a pleasure to be a small part of her golden years.

Emilia Earhart actually lived here, having owned a home right off one of the greens on the North side of the course and property. I have a Hoover Dam of small tales to tell about my few years at Lakeside, and will do so over time, but to avoid any more overflow for now, let me get to the second part of this story.

Each year the club hosts the annual Jim Murray Sportswriters Golf Tournament. I was scheduled in for my usual early afternoon to closing shift, but due to the tournament volume and activity, I came in at 1:00 pm instead of the normal 2:00 pm. Here I am, hired on as the only long-haired (at the time) black sheep of the staff family, apropos of their nature to bring someone in from the cold, a dark horse with a foot and a half-long mane, but kept tied back and clean, staying at my best behavior for some acceptance to prove myself worthy, not wanting the members to misperceive my capabilities. I was able to win them over with my professionalism, experience and knowledge behind the bar.

Starting in the morning and ending in the late afternoon, there were players who had well-finished the course when I arrived in the bar for my shift, hanging out in the clubhouse and men's bar. Kenny, the bar manager, was in back choosing wines from the cellar for some of the members dinners. Bruce was out on the course with the liquor/bar cart, and Reyes went on a long break as I took over the bar. It's a 25-30 foot bar with a service bar hatch connected to the dining area in the next room over, so I'm keeping a peripheral eye on the waiters and managers to the right.

I made a few drinks for some members and guests who popped in the bar after showering in the locker room, as well as others who were in and out from the course. I always know when actor Jack Nicholson is on the greens as his playing partner/friend comes into the bar and orders a couple cold Dr. Pepper cans with large roadie cups filled with ice. Jack's a Pepper! He even put a private review of the club and course up online some years back. It says "One of the best in Los Angeles. Great traditional course. Small, quick greens. Great place to see celebs."

So I'm there behind the bar for less than a half an hour, and as I walk down to the far left side of the bar to put some of the cigar boxes back that were left out. I turn back around facing the front of the bar and where the big screens are, I slow down to a stop, doing a visual pan of the entire room and through the far windows of the adjacent room where members were playing poker. Looking back to the left and to a round table in the deep middle of the main room, I look at the side of this person's face sitting there alone, re-adjusted my eyes and did a double-take, as it was a bit dim lit, and I'll be damned if it wasn't Joe Namath.

He seemed to be waiting for somebody, but after a couple minutes he looked back over to the bar and noticed I was there doing whatever, maybe looking at the sports page for a quick minute or so while keeping my eye out. He got up and walked right over to me and introduced himself. I did the same, we shook hands, and he ordered an Absolut on-the-rocks with no fruit. Catching my breath while preparing his drink without dropping the glass, I brought it over to him, serving it up over a Lakeside cocktail napkin, and we ended up having about a 15-20 minute conversation nearly uninterrupted.

Awesome! I'm chatting with an NFL legend. We talked a little about the club's history, how his golf game went, and I let him know that not only did I grow up watching the Jets with my dad as our favorite team, but in high school I had read his 1970 book in the library, titled "I Can't Wait Until Tomorrow 'cause I get better looking every day". Back then, he was drinking Johnnie Walker Red. We talked about his Super Bowl III game against the Baltimore Colts in 1969, and also mentioned to him that I was named after Kyle Rote, who was in the broadcast booth with Curt Gowdy, but in his day on the field used to play for the New York Giants.

He loved it! What a great guy to hang out and speak with. He was so open and laid back, in no hurry. We laughed with each other, and I got to see a close-up of that great Broadway Joe smile. Towards the end, he had finished his drink right at about the time that his golfing partner on the day had come into the bar. We shook hands and thanked each other for the chat, and they took off. The next day I called my dad to let him know that I got to meet and talk with Joe, and he couldn't believe it. He was so happy to hear it.

The day was filled with sports people walking around the property, not too many came into the bar area though, but one member that I spoke with on occasion who is an executive at Warner Brothers told me that one of his golfing partners was MLB pitcher Randy

Johnson. Later in the day, USC college baseball coaching legend Rod Dedeaux came in and up to the bar, who was a member along with his son, Justin. I walk over to greet him and he says "Hey Tiger", and asked me to get him a juice or a club soda, I can't remember exactly now. He uses a cane, but it's made out of a baseball bat which is autographed by many of his college players that made it to the big leagues. Bruce had told me about it before, and I finally got the chance to see it up close, as Rod placed it on top of the bar.

He got a kick out of the fact when I told him I used to go to all the San Diego Padres pre-season games with my dad when they were held in Yuma, Arizona, which is where I grew up from the ages of 7-19, including seeing Dave Kingman in his rookie year with the San Francisco Giants, among so many other greats of the time. Much later I found out that he had actually played a couple games with the Brooklyn Dodgers in 1935, before his back gave out and couldn't continue in the Majors. Rod passed away in 2006 at the age of 91.

By the end of the night and my shift, I closed up the bar, walked out to my truck, grabbed my putter and a few balls, and went back to the front of the clubhouse where the putting green is, and hit a bunch around while the lights were still on. What a day! It pretty much made my month, if not my year . . .

8

IN THE HOOD

I usually book almost any gig in my work calendar. I'm not too choosy with where and who for the most part, unless I actually have a choice if more than one gig comes in for the same date, though I do have some trippy road phobia about trekking over to Pasadena. I'd rather avoid the opposite end of the valley from where I live, but I've surrendered to a few in the past. It depends on the time I need to be at the gig for set-up vs. traffic stress, along with the fact that my truck isn't the newest kid on the block anymore. I also won't drive to Orange County. Just isn't worth the hassle. L.A. is so spread out, it's best to make the destinations easy on myself whenever I can.

One afternoon about 6 years ago I get a call from Tabi Cooper at Tender Bartenders, who I still work with today for private bar events. She knows me well enough to know I can be meticulous about the details and particulars of a gig beforehand, so I'm more aware of what I'm walking into. I like to look and operate as a professional behind the bar for the guests, no matter where it is so, knowing as much in advance is always a plus, as the client can be putting their event together over a period of weeks sometimes.

Tabi mentioned this party is for a 21-year old kid who just graduated from Architectural school at Cal State Irvine. I said "Cool, where's it at ?". She says "In East L.A., and East of the 110 Freeway from what the address looks like". She was right. I checked in both the Thomas Map Guide and on Mapquest, and I'd be entering the aging streets behind and South of Downtown.

This felt a bit risky for a white boy like me to drive into, and the area made me think for a few minutes. As a bit of a chance-taker myself mainly out of interest for widening experiences, as well as the need for paying the bills being an always present driving force, I reluctantly said yes, and so it was on. Luckily, the call came in a couple weeks prior to the party, so it gave me the time I needed to find the proper mental gear with which to walk in with. I knew they were renting a 6-foot bar and back table, and getting the full beverage delivery from John & Pete's in Hollywood, so I wasn't going to be the first one entering the old war zones, so to speak. If anything, I'd get a call en route if something was wrong, so I could turn back if necessary.

The day came. I exited off the 110 and made a left heading East towards and past Washington Boulevard.

It was heavy dusk so I had to pay close attention to the directions and street signs to avoid getting lost by taking a wrong turn, or turns. Eventually coming up on the street, I made a right turn and slowly rolled into the hood squinting my eyes to hopefully see the correct address and house while paying close attention to this area and it's extremely narrow neighborhood roads, where parking on the street was almost non-existent, everything was so tight together with spaces taken, and cars just made it worse. Here I am just trying to get my truck off the road, and having a hard time doing so. It always rubs my pet peeve when parking is a pain in the ass. That's why I don't live in Hollywood!

Pulling into the half a spot left available in the Volkswagon Bus-thin driveway of the home, I could finally get off the road and out of sight from any potential watchers. I'm glad it was dark for that reason alone. As my truck over the years has been vandalized, but never stolen, on five different occasions in its 23 years hauling me in various places of work except for one time. There was a built-in paranoia that I was definitely increasing the chances to make it six on this one-off gig. Not something you want to have in the back of your mind while working, but with 50-60 people showing up for the party, it actually decreases the probability of occurrence. I needed a drink at this point to ease my mind.

Knocking on the door with my bar kit over the shoulder, I was greeted by Adrian and his girlfriend, Lisa. They were very nice. Before they showed me to the back yard, they told me I could park the truck all the way into and on the front lawn. What a relief! Locating the bar area and the product and ice that had been dropped off beforehand, I just buried myself in putting the entire bar together and ready for pour with a half-an-hour to spare so I could have a drink and a smoke to calm down the mind while I was changing shirts and listening to the Dodger game on the truck radio. If anything felt like a long, hot summer, it was now, this moment.

They had hired a DJ, who arrived while I was in the front yard, reversing into the driveway with his van to unload. At this point, I felt that if something was going to happen in a bad way during the evening, at least I had some company. Next time, maybe I will consider Pasadena!

With the dance floor tiled and fit in place, we were pretty much ready to go for the night. The back yard wasn't exactly green with envy, part of the ground looking like tetherball was in Game 5 of a best of 7, and with another patch of dirt to the right and over from the bar, I was hoping those areas weren't going to raise too much dust in the air. A low power line criss-crossing the sky above the yard put things even more in question, and I found myself trouble-shooting the scene in auto-pilot mode with situations of the unknown. I was ready to get the drink-pouring underway, get the party started with guests arriving any minute, just to help the time go by a bit quicker.

The DJ was pretty much keeping his head down setting up the audio equipment in his staging area on the opposite corner of where my bar was stationed at. I had everything I needed. The beers and wines were chilled and the cocktails ready to prep. The music started, people were coming in and finding their way to the bar, and I was pouring in no time, making drinks like a machine for hours on end with hardly a break in between. The crowd turned out to be cool for the most part, though later in the evening there were a couple guys that got a little wild after having a few, but it didn't take away from the party. I was making a lot of Kamikaze's and Adios's, some martini drinks, the regular mixed drinks, and plenty of beer moved as well. We had a pony keg that I had tapped earlier, and after bleeding the line to check its unsettled (foam) level, it also ended up to be ready come game time.

Depending on what party or event I'm working determines if there will be a tip jar on the bar or not. There are times when the clients prefer to tip you at the end of the night. Happily, this night ended up hitting on both. Having a tip jar on this bar worked out well for me. Any middle-class party usually turns out that way, which is a good thing, as they tip better than the rich by a landslide. Though I have and work for rich clients who are generous, they are few and far between. But my fee or hourly pay usually makes up for it most of the time, so it's all good.

During the middle of the party and a pause in the music and dancing, Adrian's best friend received the microphone from the DJ and began to speak about all of them being here to honor the graduation of Adrian. The crowd broke out in a big cheer and you could see Adrian being hugged and high-fived by all his friends and family. It was a beautiful thing to see from someone who grew up in this part of town. I couldn't be happier for him. He came over to the bar and I congratulated him, and then put a beer and a shot in front of him, and myself!

I needed to get buzzed that night. It helped smoothen my rough edges and arc my personality towards the important task at hand, which is to provide great service with a happy attitude. I had people during the night hang out for periods of time at and around the back bar, so I engaged in many a chat.

There were so many cute Latino girls at the party, I had to watch myself at keeping a slight communicado distance from them to avoid raising any smoke from the homeys, as the girls flirted with me at the bar almost all night, in front of their boyfriends of course! But I'm good at balancing that act so the guys know I'm cool and not going to start any shit. This really isn't the place where I want my tombstone.

The party went late, ending somewhere close to 2:00 am. Around midnight my dog ears heard gunshots from some other street in the nearby area which raised the hair on the back of my neck. The one thing we didn't want is for the police to show up and knock on the door at any hour of the night, as the sensing possibility loomed of a few guys in the festivities could be packing. All went without any trouble, though something felt close! I was breaking down the bar and getting the unused product ready for John & Pete's to pick up on Sunday or Monday, then putting my bar kit back together and doing final cleanup. I met up with Adrian and Lisa near the back door of the house to collect my fee, and they tipped me on top of that for doing a great job. Awesome! The night turned out safe and sound . . . and profitable!

With the warmer than cool air out that night, the gig became a sweat along with your basic fatigue at the end. With my kit and tubs over my shoulder, I walked around the house and to the front yard to start loading in the truck, getting the shirt off my back, and figuring out how I'm going to back the truck up and out of the front yard lawn without hitting the fence or some other thing I didn't see. That's all I needed was another strategic task to handle right then. A couple of the partygoers had dropped my tailgate and were sitting down talking with one another. That was cool, actually, as at that time I realized that I didn't need to worry about not having my truck in my constant peripheral vision while I was working the bar.

Lighting a smoke and back on the street with the front yard damage-free, I now had to navigate my way back in reverse map direction through the dark back streets of East L.A. in the middle of the night/morning for about 10 minutes, praying not to get lost, and get back on the 110 to the 5 to the 134 to the 101 . . . to home.

Overall, a good night! I made it through another mystery gig, this one of a riskier potential than normal.

9

BLUE HIGHWAY

Taking a few weeks off after leaving the Black Angus in late 1987, where the first half of that time I was out of town, I ended up getting a bar job right next door at Bombay Bicycle Club, though I was searching around in a few different areas to preferably consider. Sometimes you just take what's on the table at the moment and move on, but I continued the search and worked on-call for the Registry Hotel in Universal City and back at the Castaways up on the mountain in the foothills of Burbank. This gave me a taste of what it was like to bartend in more than one venue at the same time. It was good, felt more secure and removed the reliability on just one workplace for income to get by.

Bombay was a very busy bar and restaurant, both in the afternoon and the evening, though unlike the Angus and Bobby McGee's, it didn't have a nightclub for dancing within it. What it did have was a large regular crowd, and a big 26-seat circular bar basically in the middle of everything. Good and convenient placement for the customers and the many waiters on the floor for lunch and dinner. It also had a 2 for 1 happy hour from 11:00am - 7:00pm on Monday through Friday, hence the business volume!

After some months, one of the bartenders left for a new job that she had been working on getting for some time, in an editing production facility for film and television. Everyone was happy for her, and I became the recipient of more shifts. No complaints! I had just enough room in my schedule for it while still holding on to the other on-call jobs. This was one of those rare places where you made good regular money in both the day and night positions behind the bar. What was tough were the scheduling glitches here and there where I'd close one night and open up the next morning, really screwing with your normal sleeping hours. Though you don't want to be showing signs of fatigue when on-the-job, most of the time you got away with it by just normally being wired with the energy of the work and the communication from all the people you're in contact with during any given high-volume shift.

The regulars were like the Motley Crue of the movie industry, behind-the-camera types working in lights and sound, as well as many other business owners in the area, construction of all sorts and what have you. It was a quite a fun, joke-telling crowd at the bar. Johnny Magnus, the great radio host and personality would come in and hang out with us. There were plenty of known actors and personalities who came in for lunch or dinner, as it was so conveniently located near, yet just off the beaten path of the studios.

Then there was Lucky, when he was in from Las Vegas, who was the best joke-teller in the bunch. He was in charge of most of the security at the hotels at the time, but didn't care to live there all that much. He and I spoke quite a bit. He must have noticed something in my disposition, as he would occasionally ask me if I'd be interested in bartending the private card games in the Nevada desert, or bartending for the casinos in general. He certainly had the connections to make something happen, but in another twist of irony, I was dating a girl who had just moved to L.A. from Vegas, where she had been a professional show dancer, and though I wasn't quite willing to give that up, the thought of living in Las Vegas didn't have a strong appeal to me either. I was interested in flying up on-call when needed, but that didn't pan out. They probably needed me to be a bit more convenient than that.

Dana, one of the regular bartenders at Bombay for some years, had gotten into an argument with the managers over some damn thing or another, and unfortunately following an unexpected three-day suspension, he ended up either getting fired or just didn't come back at all. I don't think any of us really found out the ruckus, which is abnormal in itself considering the work environment. Needless to say, they had to hire another bartender. This time they went with someone fresh instead of previously known, like myself.

From back East, they hired a big guy named Michael Eagleton, who had some good experience working many of the busy bars in Florida. We worked as the dynamic duo behind the bar during the busy day shifts, and grew a popular following. Having the nights off for the most part, we would at times hang out and go do something, whether it be a Laker game, a concert, a theatre-stage show downtown, or whatever.

At one point, a bunch of us at the club were searching around for new living quarters. I came across an ad for renting a huge house way up in the Granada Hills, just off the 405 freeway in the Northwest part of the valley, for $2400 a month. It was crazy for us to consider, but with 5 bedrooms, 3 baths, 2 living rooms, a rock steam room inside the house, a full tennis court, a custom-built man cave with a fireplace if you can picture that, and of course a pool. It became, from a party standpoint, difficult to pass up. Surprisingly, five of us actually came together and did it. With three of the female waiters from Bombay on the West side of the house, Michael and I took the other two larger bedrooms on the East side.

Though we had several small get-togethers depending on our hours off, there was one time where we felt that we better have a big party, not knowing how long we were going to actually last in the house as a cohesive unit of five. It was month-to-month, so we avoided signing a lease of any kind, as the Santa Monica owners also had the house on the market for sale at the same time. A nice built-in defense mechanism for us! It was appropriate for the case when you have a group of young renters potentially going in different directions, though we all worked out of the same hub.

It took us some time to switch the green light into a go and put the party together, but we did it. We had small flyers out to the staff and some choice customers from the bar, including Max, who owned a woodshop business in the industrial district nearby. He donated a custom-built 8-foot portable bar that he threw together in no time, which was so awesome for him to do for us. The house didn't have a bar inside, but having more of the party outside was our main priority anyway, considering the possibility of 100-200 guests, it was better for the bar to be out near the pool.

One of the girls got the food appetizers in place, I was putting the music and sound system together, and a bunch of us pitched in, as well as other side donations, for the liquor, mixers, kegs, cups and ice. I even rented a Sparkletts water cooler and filled it with close to three gallons of a flavored specialty Kamikaze, and let it sit overnight to get nice and cold. There was a new development of housing construction just across the street, and one night Michael and I got high on some great weed with the girls and a couple other friends, and we decided to temporarily heist the just-emptied and cleaned port-o-potty for our mid-afternoon/early evening Sunday soiree, so the inside bathrooms wouldn't be bombarded. I had the truck, we had the might, it was done.

One of the cocktail waitresses at the club, Jennie, was also a lead singer and guitarist in an all-female rock band that would perform a couple times a month in some of the clubs in Hollywood. She was letting her girlfriends know about the party, and let us know that we may have a surprise guest appearance, a very popular rock n' roll artist who did some background vocals on their album.

That was cool! But it didn't weigh heavy on us, as most of the time those type of things kind of fall through.

Then came the day. We were pretty much all ready and at that point were just hoping that the expected people would show up. We gave specific directions on paper as it was up in the hills, didn't want everyone to get lost and give up. It slowly became a great turnout as the party was over about an 8-hour span or so. A great thing happened when many of our customers who showed up let us know in advance that they wanted to tend bar, so they took short-shift turns, and we had the bar covered so Michael and I, and other bartenders there didn't have to pull any time.

It was the summer, so we had longer hours of daylight. About 3 hours into the party and close to 100 people gathered and having a great time all over this sprawling property with a canyon overlook on top of everything else, we heard a slew of motorcycles come up the road, parking at the entrance. Michael was guarding the gate at the time and welcoming guests. I went up to my room on the second floor to adjust the sound levels of the music. A minute later Michael comes in the side door entrance to his room on the third floor, above mine. I then heard his linebacker body come down the stairs and into my room, and he said "Guess who's here ?".

It was Billy Idol, some of his band and a couple riding friends. It had to have been six of them. My jaw dropped for a moment in how crazy it was for him to be at our party. We started smiling and laughing. Our surprise guests had arrived after all. But I hadn't seen Jennie and her friends yet. Michael proceeded to do bongs with Billy and the gang back up in his room after I initially went up with him for a proper greeting. I reluctantly had to pass, as I didn't want to be too blitzed at the function I co-created, but knew Sally my girlfriend was showing up sometime in the evening and I wanted to be coherent. I knew Michael could handle the host position better at that time anyway.

They all made it downstairs and out to the party in the back yard, where several people couldn't believe their eyes, but the music was rocking at a nice volume so luckily there wasn't any strange moments of silence. Billy and crew hung out near the beer kegs, and were at the party for a good 2-3 hours. Eventually I went over and hung out for a minute. They were a gracious but high group of guys with sunglasses on, as I, making it easier to chat a little without the need for direct red eye contact. I asked Billy if he had heard about Jennie and friends showing up. Unknown to me at the time, he said that she got called into work.

A bummer of a turn, but at least they still showed up. That was very cool of them, and they had a Sunday destination on the bikes for a while that was only 15-20 miles from Hollywood. I had also complemented him on the background vocals of a song he performed on the Joni Mitchell album titled "Night Ride Home". He was appreciative and surprised that I would know of it, as it's one of those obscure things that can go by without notice.

The party continued on close to 11:00 pm, but guests had shuffled in and out at all hours of the event, so there was never too many at one time. Sally had arrived between 9:00 and 10:00 pm, which was perfect timing for things cooling down. Everybody had a blast. Plenty of swimmers in the pool. Tim and Ronnie, my ex-Angus co-bartenders were playing night H-O-R-S-E on the lighted basketball side of the tennis court, where people were nearby playing over-the-net Frisbee. Then my basketball bounces over the high fence and into the canyon, never to be found again. Above all, the cave was probably the most popular of attractions. People took turns just hanging out in it.

No harm, no falls, no accidents, and everyone got home safe. The party was talked about at the club for weeks if not months after. And who else can say they had Billy Idol show up to their party . . .

10

ACCESS ALL AREAS

One of the many on-call outfits I found myself connected to was bartending at the famous Hollywood Palladium. From 2002-2006 I was part of the bar staff that worked a wide variety of events during that stretch of time; concerts, movie rap parties, fashion shows, fundraisers, corporate events, celebrity parties, award shows, private parties, political events, auto shows, charity balls, New Years Eve, and the annual tattoo convention called "The Inkslingers Ball".

At a cost of $1.6 million, the concert/dance hall with a capacity of 4,000 opened in October of 1940 with a dance featuring Tommy Dorsey and his Orchestra and band vocalist Frank Sinatra. Aside from hosting the Emmy's, Grammy's and Golden Globes over the years, plenty of music legends made their way to the Palladium stage including the Stones, Beach Boys, Led Zeppelin, Bowie, the Grateful Dead, Bob Dylan, Stevie Wonder, Madonna, Barbara Streisand, and hundreds of other major artists past and present. Even the Jimi Hendrix Experience performed at a week-long event in the venue, called Pop Expo 69'.

A host of big bands performed there during the popular years of that music in the 40's and 50's, and during WWII, the Palladium hosted radio broadcasts featuring Betty Grable greeting servicemen's song requests. The Tito Puente Orchestra performed regularly from 1957-1977 to sold-out houses. In 1961, it also became the home of the long-running Lawrence Welk Show. During this period, President Kennedy spoke at a Democratic party dinner there, and in 1965 Martin Luther King was honored by city officials recognizing his Nobel Peace Prize.

The Los Angeles Times publisher Norman Chandler funded the construction of the art deco palace that was built where the original Paramount lot once stood, on Sunset Boulevard between Argyle and El Centro avenues. It was designed by Gordon Kaufmann, architect of the L.A. Times building, the Santa Anita Racetrack, the Greystone Mansion, and was also the architect for the Hoover Dam.

So many unbelievable nights of entertainment at this historical venue located in the heart of Hollywood, and wishing I was a vampire bartender so I could live 150 years and witness it all, if I had started way back then.

Do to my experience and level of bar knowledge, I was thankful to the management for putting me into the busiest spots throughout the venue. There has to be a good six built-ins and another half-dozen portables placed where needed, from the entrance all the way to the top. I've pretty much worked all of them at one time or another, but on real busy or sold-out events, I was usually stationed with Heidi upstairs in the VIP Bar. Henry, the bar manager and on-premise security live-in ghost companion was kind and smart enough to take advantage of what he had in his bar staff, which had to have been 30-40 people on-call.

Heidi was the lead with the most tenure at about 15 years, and I basically came in as the designated hitter wherever they needed me most. Built for speed and pace of ring, I was a money player for the most part, a human drink machine, but I also enjoyed and excelled in the spotlight. The managers knew I had their backs as I had been a bar and nightclub manager at previous times in the past, and had no interest in their positions. We just needed to make sure the barbacks had their shit together, especially with moving the kegs and CO_2 tanks in place behind the bars so they could settle, and not blowing or dying at the wrong times.

With Alan, the GM, we never knew what mood he was going to be in when bartenders arrived at staggered call times, hot or cold, or on the warpath about something. Let's just say his on-the-job intensity was pressure-raising. When you're dealing with a who's who of promoters and connivers over the phone setting up event dates, deposits, guarantees, sound & light specifics, gate receipts and whatever other paperwork involved, you can imagine pulling your hair out with endless decision-making and compromises till the deal is done, and setting up the details to properly execute the event, hoping nothing goes astray.

All we wanted to do was come in and kick ass behind the bar, as that was effectively our job, but other dramas could stream in and bleed on our shoulders at times taking us off our game depending on who we're working with and next to at any given bar station. Sometimes the slightest infraction could potentially lead to being fired for some of the younger bartenders, or practicing the new standard of just being written off the schedule in the attempt to avoid a lazy one from walking to the unemployment line. Certain people just wouldn't get called in again. This type of thing mainly happened to some of the stray cat bartenders who could half-care less about what they were doing, eventually becoming their demise.

On this one particular night in 2002, the rock band Audioslave was performing a sold-out show during a full tour in support of their debut album. Knowing close to a month in advance and a long-time fan of singer Chris Cornell, I was anxious to see the show, well, more like hear the show, as the VIP Bar doesn't offer much in visibility. However, I was also interested in getting there early to not only see the soundcheck, but to walk around to the back of the stage.

With my badge over my shirt so no one from security would stop me for a Q & A session, my timing of arrival worked perfectly. I walked in back and it was empty of any casual lingering. I stepped up and onto the rear of the stage and they began jamming on a few songs to get the levels right for the sound guys. It was like loud heaven. Though I had my earplugs with me, I didn't put them in. Brad Wilk's drum kit sounded like thunder and lightning. Cornell was at the front of the stage belting for the engineer, and I just stood there mesmerized for 10 minutes. With Tom Morello shredding on guitar and Tim Commerford on bass, there wasn't any letting up for the sound check. They rocked it!

Looking in back of me every minute or two to make sure the coast was still clear, about the third or fourth time I saw Alan walk by. He looked up at me for a moment, I gave him a happy grin, and he graciously continued on without asking me off the stage. That was very cool of him, as normally the opposite would be expected to happen.

After setting up the VIP Bar with Heidi, we were ready to roll. It soon got packed up in the area, as well as the whole place, so her and I were cranking the drinks out rough and tumble. Alan would always come up to her and get a cocktail for himself, made with his favorite vodka, Ciroc. As long as he was over there, I was fine. For some reason, bartenders here are always waiting for something to go wrong, ahead of time, just so we can properly defend ourselves. The energy with this many people basically in a gigantic club atmosphere can rev up to a volatile stage, so there's always watchers, and we feel them.

With concerts, you usually have opening acts before the headliner. This was no exception, so we would get rushes between bands along with our normal crowd of people in the general area who were in and out of the bar when they wanted to look down at the stage. We were located up in the East balcony, but the overlook was sensational. The night and the show went great in the old L.A. landmark once again! When Audioslave came on and did an encore of Rush's "Working Man", I couldn't believe it. It was awesome. Heidi's take on Cornell is that "He can do no wrong!"

Later in the night after cleaning and closing down the bars and turning in our banks of cash in the office upstairs in another part of the building facing Sunset Strip, I was walking back down the long staircase and across the huge dance floor towards one of the double-doors at the rear of the building on the West side of the stage to the outside parking lot. As I was let out, to the right of me about 10 feet as I was walking by, Chris Cornell was signing autographs through a chain link fence as the other members of the band were waiting in the limo nearby with the door open. Kind of strange! Why weren't they out signing their CD as well? I just can't see Cornell as an autographing bogart. Maybe they only had one sharpie between the four of them!

After all, it wasn't an arranged sit down thing, so it was very generous of Chris to take the time. The rest of the band members in the back of the car had expressions looking like they just wanted to get back to the hotel, though I think Morello lives in L.A., and Cornell was known to have a home in Beverly Hills. And who would have known that in 2008 while bartending on-call in Calabasas at an Italian restaurant called The Riviera, that Brad Wilk and his spouse were regular customers there, who always ordered a bottle of Opus 1 with dinner.

Oh well . . . that's rock n' roll at the Hollywood Palladium . . .

11

GRAMMY PARTY –
SUNSET PLAZA DRIVE

During the first week in February of 2004, I was asked to be the bar manager for an after-Grammy Awards party given by hip-hop artists, Outkast. Days before the event, several people met at the site where the party was to take place and discussed bar placements, beverage requirements, ice storage, and many other things one can imagine for a get-together the size of about 1200 guests.

Being present for this meeting, we also went on a walk-through of this spectacular home way up Sunset Plaza Drive in the hills above Sunset Boulevard, where we were told the place used to be owned a long time ago by W.C. Fields. Interesting piece of trivia. A house with four floors, as well as a convenient elevator to all of them. At the very top there are two incredible catwalks that take themselves quite a distance against the cliff walls, connected to the rooftop of the house. A gazebo, fire pit, a small telescope observatory, and the incredible view of Los Angeles located on the same level gave us an indication of how great the party would be.

A private event for the music and entertainment industry, it was a sizeable task to accomplish. We were initially hoping that the weather would change by the weekend to something good, in place of the clouds and the scent of rain that were above our heads just five days before. Therefore, to take precautions the tennis court at the main/top floor level was completely tented. It was an inside/outside party, and the tennis court was going to play a big part in it. This was a scary if not shaky thought, as it was held up by long wooden beams drilled into the mountain side and cemented.

Considering how many potential partygoers were going to be out there at any given time vs. the body weight times how many people, along with the bars, a Red Bull bar, ice, product, the DJ stage, other equipment, and the dance floor right in the middle of the court, it made a few of us think about safety concerns. If the whole thing were to collapse and fall down the mountain side due to the floor pounding with both sound and weight, I was going to make sure and be at another part of the property, or at the very least taking a leaping grasp to the semi-connected high chain-link fencing at the rear. As far as exits on the court, there was only one way out.

On the day of the event, which was basically a split-shift 15 hour work stretch for me, there were deliveries of many things, delegating the drop-off guys to where products needed to go, as well as lifting a lot myself to help out and get my hands dirty, gaining their respect. I had the beverage product all in a one hub area in front and back of the court fence, needing to further issue out measured amounts of product for each of the bar areas and get it all moved over to each back bar. Thankfully I had a few other hands helping out.

Since this place had many levels and steps up and down, it was the most exhaustive schlepping-of-product experience I've been in the middle of to date. Though we had 2-wheel dollies that were of definite need, the outside of the house had virtually no gradual ramps for ease of simply rolling the dolly up and down the various floors. This is the worst part of the staging of an event. It is also extra time consuming, that is usually not taken into consideration during set-up hours. With a party this size and scope, it's best to get it all done with plenty of time to spare, instead of the crew running around frantic at the last minute or as guests were arriving, especially with the wiring of the sound systems, where they had their own power generator. Luckily, we still finished in good time. I got there early to get working on anything I could get done and out of the way, and it helped, to get it out of their way too.

Diageo supplied/donated the whole kit and caboodle for the party as far as beverages for the bars; liquor, beer, wine, mixers, juices, and waters. What a deal! It was also a good spot to unload some variety of flavored Smirnoff inventory, as well as 20 cases of Red Stripe beer. But hey, it's free! Chef Yealang Smith took care of the food end for the entire night, so it was all coming together; Food, Beverage, Music, Entertainment.

Since this was a fully shuttled and name on list affair, they had these cool, custom mini-roadsters at the front gate drop-off to take people up the steep hill to the house. Through the bright lights of the Paparazzi walk and pic-take, you entered the second level of the home and worked your way up. This property was a physical workout to put a big party like this together, but all departments pulled through, as the day was warm and we knew the evening was going to be a beautiful night. Driving back to the house after taking a break with a few hours to spare, it was an exciting energy to start the rest of the night with, knowing that everything was in place and ready to roll.

With six bars in four different places, including a small Cognac and Liqueur bar in an upper part of the house called the Moroccan Room, which was a great crib to hang out and lounge in, and smoke. The three different DJ's were located in the Main room, the tented court, and another outside on the entrance side of the house next to the pool and Jacuzzi, so there was hot music everywhere in the air. Along with gaming tables, the stage was set for this total party pad. This house at the time, whoever owned and/or managed it, was renting it out on a semi-regular basis for various parties that came calling.

As I was roaming around up and down the entire night, making sure the staff were in rhythm and had everything they needed, I had to also stay on the barbacks to know that they were keeping up with ice and product demands at the bars, as with bars it's always product in and product out. There were freezers delivered and set-up in the garage area, where we had over 2,000 pounds of ice stocked. That was beautiful. I didn't want 40 50-lb. bags stacked and slowly melting all over the carport area throughout a good 7 hours, and longer for any unused.

The cocktail waitresses were split in the three main bar areas, but I left them alone for the most part just to do their own thing. I understood where their motivation was - $, so it was better to have them simply manage themselves. Chris had the food waiters and bussers, and since I knew and had worked with him on many other occasions, I didn't need to get in his way. He was a strong and fair person to have on-board, so I had faith in him to keep an equal eye.

Tabi had showed up to party and was there for awhile before she found me. We eventually made our way up to the Moroccan Room and had a drink and a smoke together just outside the room at the very tip top of the home. Great overlook of Hollywood at night. I was so adrenalized for sound and vision at that point, no amount of drink was going to take me over or slow me down. That's just what happens when you do what I do at events like this. It helps that I'm a completist, so I'm usually amped to the finish line, however far off.

Notables I ran into during some of the busy, tight areas of walking space, of which the house was packed, and pretty much the tennis court as well, were Lennox Lewis, David Alan Grier, and Jessica Simpson and Nick Lachey. They were sitting together in a small loveseat for two inside the double-screen door of the house at the top floor going out to the court. There were plenty of others I'm sure, some I know of and many I don't know who they were. I didn't see Andre and Big Boi, but heard they were going to arrive at some point in time during the night.

There were a lot of crazy outfits that guests were wearing, which made it look like a bit of a masquerade party. With this many peeps all together at an annual Hollywood music industry gathering, you see all kinds invited, and it's designed that way. With girls walking around with next-to-nothing on, and the sex circus in attendance, it was nice to know we had a professional fully-staffed security detail. After a while, I started taking good use of the elevator, which increased the destination pace a little better instead of going the long way around the house or the thoroughfare through the mainstay and big house bar section at the top floor.

Thanks to L.A.'s Tender Bartenders for casting a special selection of bartenders, cocktail waitresses, food servers, barbacks, and bussers that held together well and did a great job. The party turned out to be spectacular, with all-night appetizers from the kitchen that were simply amazing. If this house was a night club, I'd want to tend bar here, just for something different!

It's 5:00 am. Barely a soul around except for what's left of mine and a few other working stiffs. These two girls, acting with some independent fashion on behalf of the party, were supposed to pay me the remaining balance before I left. Thinking they were being really slick, deliberately failed to have a check left over to write out the remainder due, close to $6000, upon completion. As I was looking over the grounds nearby for an available shank, they asked me if I'd like to take any or all of the leftover liquor product, used and unused, of which there was plenty as always.

Though I had my truck to do so, I declined, as I knew they would soon try to use it against me, ready to tell any other higher-ups (whoever the fuck they were) connected to the night's event that I took it without permission, in an attempt to justify a reason not to pay. If anyone deserved to be briskly shoved off the cliff, it was these two rookie twats for thieves. However, my only responsibility was to collect the check, it was not mine to pay. So I left without, and was to report into Tabi the following afternoon.

It was a late one, as I finally ended up leaving the premises at 5:30 am, just in time to enter the early stages of morning traffic on the way back home. So I ditched it a little bit and took Sunset all the way to the ocean drive down PCH (Pacific Coast Highway), stopped at the beach, enjoyed the sunrise and a smoke for a while, and took off through Topanga Canyon and into Woodland Hills for breakfast, and mucho sleep!

Days went by with no message response from these two little criminals, as expected. Tabi still had to pay everyone on the staff, and now she was out. I was also in charge of collecting the hours worked by everyone, and to add any extra hours worked beyond the minimum and put all the totals together for the final number and balance.

As karma and happenstance would have it from there, a month later or so, Chris Stone runs into one of the event managers that he had previously chatted with sometime during the party, in a building elevator on Wilshire Boulevard, as he was going to meet his brother at his work office. They speak about the problem of no pay, and the guy gives Chris the phone number and address of the office and person to speak with for a remedy to the issue at hand. Chris calls Tabi to let her know of the new information. She calls the office and low and behold, she gets paid a week later.

With the tardiness, Tabi tacked on another 10% for her anguish, and they agreed and paid in full. No telling what trouble the girls got into, but hopefully a lesson was learned, and that is, never try to get away without paying the floor staff.

12

I LOVE THE NIGHT . . . . . SHIFT

Every once in a while I get walled into pulling a double gig. As much as I'd like to avoid them, I also have a hard time saying no to any gigs that come in because, well, all of my bar work is on-call, and sensing the laws of karma walk very close with me, I know that if I decline on a gig for whatever reason, I'll get smacked with the loss of another one or I'll get double-booked on the same date where I can't work them both. However, the same works to benefit in the opposite way too, so I say yes to everything regardless of the stress or sleep deprivation that may occur.

This back-to-back that happened on a Friday in September of 2005, I couldn't have asked for better location convenience, especially in this area that I rarely get to anymore, as both events were Downtown. The opener was a late afternoon call time at the old L.A. Times building. The party at the Times was a reception/speaking engagement for the new Editor-in-Chief. This gig I was dialed in to work for Bar One Catering, a service out of Palos Verdes, though they work many events in the L.A. area as well as over in Orange County, which from where I reside is a bit too far off in the distance to trek, yet I enjoyed working with the outfit when they had gigs in town, as they were very fair with plenty of advance notice with booking, good pay, and it was a fun group of staff.

Parking in the ticketed lot next door and just in back of the building, I was looking forward to go inside. I became a little bit of an L.A. history buff after reading Marc Reisner's 1986 book titled Cadillac Desert – The American West and its Disappearing Water, so I was up on the Harrison Gray Otis era in and around 1900, along with The Chandler Family that followed, and the history of William Mulholland in the Department of Water and Power, and his Owens Valley Project, a 7-year construction that brought a water source from 250 miles away to a thirsty-for-growth little town back then, as at that time L.A. was only half the size of San Francisco. Think Chinatown!

The inside of the building was everything expected and more from a news and media institution, from the front entrance filled with historical material and information, and other related interests as I made my way up the elevator and to the third floor where the reception was to take place. We started setting up the bars and back bars with ice and glassware, tubs and bar tools, then filled it in with the full-bar selection of beverages that we offered for that evening's event. Though we were using long portable bars for this occasion as a way to fit comfortably in this kind of long hallway/breezeway space in the center of the floor and close to the main gathering and podium stage, they have custom built-in bars on the second floor for larger cocktail parties and the like. I'm thinking to myself "Built-in bars at The Times . . . Nice!" Who would've known?

At some point the Mayor was due to show up to be a part of the festivities, so it's always good to prepare your professional behavior behind the bar not only preferred to the client's interests, but to represent the service I was hired into work with and give the best bar performance possible. The majority of the crowd were a mix of executives, administrative personnel, and staff writers where some had their dress coats on while others still had their sleeves rolled up like they were still sitting down at their office computers finishing up a story deadline. This changing-of-the-guard formality was probably an interruption to some overachievers at the paper, but at least it wasn't happening in the middle of the day in case they were out on the beat. But we had drinks . . . . . so the pens dropped.

As the bars opened for service, we started to get busy real quick and steady from what began to resemble a multi-floor cubicle exodus of the building over to our hosted cocktail and appetizer lounge for the night. A nice ending to a shift before you go home for the weekend. As a bartender, it's all too easy to chat with people in any group that you're serving, so this was no different. You're also in natural earshot of guests talking shop or whatever, if one cares to tune in. At other times it's so close you can't get away from it, therefore it's good to just stay busy and at least look like I'm minding my own business!

When you get a new chief in the office, it's hard to know what to think at any level. It becomes a wait and see to a certain degree, but the one thing they can all agree on initially is no layoffs, positional shifting around, or title elimination. It's never a good thing to live in fear of a staff reduction. I'm hearing and looking at all these goings-on and I realize what happens here is like anywhere else. The same issues and problems no matter how high or low the workplace. Thank God I'm off the grid for the most part. It alleviates me from having to deal with that dynamic of inner workings. I don't have anything against it at all, as I've been there before, but I'm happier with the way I work now, though it's not without its own hustles and struggles. That's food and beverage for you. The second-largest employer in the U.S., and doesn't take care of its own ! Welcome to living without a net . . . . . or rather, *existing* without a net.

With the tray-passing of finger foods, there's always someone that comes back to the bar with a mouth of crumbs ordering another whiskey and ginger, as a chaser! I immediately pour a short water on the side for them as a convenience to their palate, with no particular mention as to why. He listened to me when I wasn't speaking, understanding the move in my timing and slow placement of the glass is all it takes as a silent courtesy, clearing his lips of falling flake debris just in time, as a female staff member bellied up next to him at the bar for me to pour her another glass of pinot grigio. Cocktail napkins on the bar top come in handy. I should dampen some of them though, like a KFC wet wipe, a little smoother on the skin.

The Mayor has arrived, and after a few minutes of initial greetings the introduction soon begins to gather and take place, starting with the managing editor's opening comments, soon going into the night's main course of welcoming. This is when everyone in the crowd turns a 180-degree about-face away from me and the bars, with Dean working the other bar close to 30 feet over to the right of me and on the other side of a wall. With some gigs and their potential short duration, there's more set-up and breakdown than the actual pouring and service, so it seems. Either way it's still a 5-hour minimum, and it all works out, though I do prefer more gig than schlep. After closing comments from the new Editor-in-Chief, the event stayed alive for a while but eventually people started to slowly pack it up and go, knowing the traffic home was going to be much less and more relaxing.

We finish up the van-loading of product and mobile road gear around 10:30 or so. It gave me plenty of time to get back to my truck and catch a long sit-down breather before I shape-shift into a different character for the second gig on the double-bill. My dress would go from formal black and white tux and tie to a loose and comfortable shirt top to make cocktails for a totally different hip and cool crowd . . . the vampires of L.A.

Though it would have been easier just to hop on the freeway and head further South and take the rap-around to the specific exit, I chose to use the Thomas Guide I keep in the truck to map my way through the backstreets of the once rough hood, turning out to be not that bad of an overall navigation, once I got out of the central downtown one-way street practices that require extra attention, especially for me. It brings back a bad memory from when I was 19 and working as a lot jockey in the largest Chevrolet dealership in Phoenix. I was returning a fresh body-repaired corvette to its owner downtown with another lot jockey close behind in another vehicle to give me a ride back. Not realizing I was on a one-way street, I made a left where the address was and BAM! It wasn't huge, but it was a dent, and had to go back to the fiberglass bodyman in the shop, and I felt like such an asshole. Needless to say, I avoid one-ways like the plague, even though I'm hyper-aware about it now, but every rare time I find myself on one, that 30+ year memory comes to the forefront in a millisecond.

Gig two was going to pretty much be an all-nighter. It was located in an industrial district in the back of downtown, in a big warehouse and kitchen owned by a popular Chef and Caterer in town, who used her own facility for occasional after-hours parties complete with DJ's, food and bar, and smokes. Upstairs was also her crib which was set-up quite awesome, so the property served a few purposes, home and business. They also have a sizeable parking area fenced at the front of the street, that they keep closed and utilize the space for maybe a few expensive sports cars, but mainly as the outdoor patio and hangout to the party for fresh air and for peeps who smoke a variety of tobacco and weed. This is an area where any residential is so far away that the music can be turned up loud and nobody is going to hear it even with the outdoor loading gate open to the patio.

I arrive and park on the street around midnight, in visual proximity to the door security guys who will be planted out there most of the night and into the early morning hours. I walk over with my bar pack and let them know who I am. They allow me in, and I go to the bar and start setting up my gear, soon speaking with the Chef's brother and assistant on what's going to be happening for the night, drink prices, and so on. I asked if they've got enough ice and plastic glassware, then we got into the product stock. The DJ's were setting up their sound and spin gear in the main room of the warehouse and dance floor. The ship was getting ready to take off.

Starting at 1:00 am is a cover charge at the door. We have a full bar of mixed drinks, beer and wine, and Chef puts out a large spread of various light munchies on a buffet table for the wolves of the night to devour, so we have this feel of a massive living room with a high ceiling for the party. It shifts into a dark-but-lit club atmosphere. The weather was great. It was a nice night with a slow, occasional breeze to eventually cool the sweat of the long dancers.

We charged for drinks and bottled waters, but I never did see the liquor license. Yet, with this situation someone had to be taken care of to look the other way, the trade-off being that up to 200 partiers and ecstasy poppers would be off the streets avoiding cruising trouble. Instead, we dealt with them. People would soon crowd the place after the legit clubs gave last call, and we became the happening underground groove dome in the back of downtown. For the police, it was better to have them all in one spot so they could concentrate on more important and severe matters of criminality. At least until the highways were bare, anyway.

We cranked out the drinks for hours. It's easy to lose track of time this late, so I didn't even pay attention to it. I just wanted to roll through without the minute monkey on my back, passes by quicker. It was loud inside so I had my earplugs in about half-way or just enough where they wouldn't fall out while I was constantly moving and shaking. After the first few hours of rush, I took a 15-minute break, went outside to the patio with a drink and chatted with a couple people, then walked back in through the front door entrance and over to my truck to have a quick smoke. It can get nerve-racking.

Getting back to the bar just in time as we seemed to get busy again, it then tapered off and we operated in slow-steady mode over the last couple hours of service. I was bartending with the Chef's sister, so I helped with the setting up of her well more efficiently, and she had a good time working it, but they had me there for speed and to handle the bulk of the load for the most part. As the bar slowed toward the onset of the early morning sunrise, there were still plenty of people hanging around and enjoying themselves, thankful for a place to go and exercise the rest of their energies after the midnight hour.

I did some of the main cleanup to help out, as I knew when to start fading the sails without guest notice, at a time that they soon would no longer need me. The better part of 12 hours on my feet, my arms and body were done, but my legs were fine. Like a horse, I can stand and graze for hours, as long as I'm moving. I left about 8:00 am just after getting paid in full, letting the other bartender take over and finish up the last hour or two. It was time for me to go. I slipped my sunglasses on, as my eyes have always been a little light-sensitive no matter what hours of the sun, started the engine up, and entered the exit onto the semi-quiet freeway rap-around close by with two things on my mind: breakfast and sleep, thinking to myself, there's more than one type of vampire in this town.

Por la Manana . . .

13

SHIRLEY AND MARTY

Some years back, from 2004-2006, I was the bartender for the Christmas Day parties at the home of legendary stage, film and television actress Shirley Jones, and her husband, Marty Ingels. They had recently moved over to the valley from their Beverly Hills residence, which ended up to be just 10 minutes from where I live, down the 101 freeway and South of Ventura Boulevard, about a mile up into the hills of Encino. They had decided to downsize a bit, which is always a smart thing to do in L.A. when you may not need the expanse of a larger property after the kids have gone.

In December I pretty much stay in town and keep my gig schedule open to work any day of the month, filling as many dates as I can, not always knowing how work load is going to play out in January. I do, however, try to scoot out of town in November for a week to my parents' house in Arizona for Thanksgiving, and to rest up for the busy month ahead. I like driving down to the border town in the middle of the night with very little traffic on the road, as L.A. can be hell to get out of during the day while still facing the timing issue a couple hours later of slipping through San Diego before rush hour. It's the difference between it taking five hours at night or eight hours when the sun is up. I've made that mistake before. But I like the drive through the desert.

It's always interesting to work a bar gig in the homes of stars, not that it isn't with everyday people, but you walk in with this heightened sense of awareness with who they already are, so the air can be lighter if you allow it, unless one is susceptible to getting star-struck. Thankfully for me, all the years I've worked at The Gardenia Room and other establishments had mellowed me out about that sort of thing, so I was a more seasoned fit for the task. Just don't tip over any glassware or make loud noises!

Greeting Marty and talking with him for a bit always put me in a relaxed state, as his personality was loose and quite funny to listen to and chat with. He actually had interest in my job as a private bartender and would always inquire about things and how I was doing. We got along well. The bar set-up was kind of between the kitchen and living room, a perfect space for me to get my *mise en place* going. There was plenty of food right in back of me, so I would hang and chew the stew with the kitchen help for the better part of the event. It was a mid-afternoon arrival with a guest count around 40-50 people including family and friends, which was a nice size group, so I wouldn't be busting too hard after the initial rush, considering I had just worked the night before on Christmas Eve for the annual party at Dale and Eugene's up on Mulholland.

Shirley came downstairs and into the kitchen to make sure everything was getting prepared. I remember first meeting her. It was like looking at my mom, blond-haired and beautiful. She was gracious and kind, so I couldn't help but to feel right at home after awhile. I almost felt like one of the sons. You never want to get too comfortable though. It's always best to stay professional about the job, and realize that I'm just a hired hand for the day, keeping my communications in check. But it's difficult to remain being the stoic pro behind the bar when Marty is around.

The family and grandchildren would usually be the first ones to arrive, which included Shirley's three sons with her late husband, the great character and musical stage actor, Jack Cassidy. So Shaun, Patrick and Ryan and the wives and kids would show up, but David was never present. Though his mother was Jack's first wife, the actress Evelyn Ward, he and Shirley have always remained close friends, He was living out of state at the time, I think doing shows in Las Vegas, so he probably spent the holiday with his wife and family at home instead of travelling long distance.

All the other guests would soon arrive and before you knew it we had a party happening. With Shirley knowing so many people in the movie business, I was curious to see who was going to walk through the front door and eventually making their way to the bar. I remember Bernie Kopell from The Love Boat showing up, as well as the host of the 60's/70's game show The Hollywood Squares, Peter Marshall, and the great actor, comedian and impersonator, Frank Gorshin, who played "The Riddler" in the original Batman television series, and was in one of my favorite movies when I was a kid, playing the role of Iggy in "That Darn Cat!". I asked Frank if he ever did an impersonation of Christopher Walken, and he said "No, I never have, but he would be interesting. I don't do hundreds of people. I've always kept it to around 50 or so". Some of those would include James Cagney, Al Jolson, Cary Grant, and Edward G. Robinson.

Everyone was having cocktails and enjoying themselves, catching up with friends they haven't seen for some time. I made some expected classic cocktails for this crowd and age group, which I always enjoy preparing. The Old Fashioned, the Side Car, Manhattans, Rob Roys, Tom Collins, a Gibson, a Belvedere Martini up with a twist for Shirley, as well as Cosmo's and Lemon Drops for the Cassidy wives, along with other simple mixed drinks and a nice selection of Cabernet's and Chardonnay's, and Heineken and Amstel Light for the brews. In fact, while growing up, Shirley's father owned a brewing company in Pennsylvania.

Whenever Shaun came to the bar, I was basically looking at the singer of the hit single "Hey Deanie, won't you come out tonight", as I remembered it from working in record stores when I was a teenager. Today, he's an accomplished television writer and producer, having made his way through the ranks of Hollywood over the years. I'm just finishing watching the last two discs in my Netflix queue of his 2006 television series "Invasion". He lives even closer to me, just over in the gated equestrian community of Hidden Hills, where many notables live. I still work private parties in there to this day for a variety of clients.

Patrick is an actor and stage performer, and Ryan is a set dresser for many television shows. It's quite a talented family overall. There's a beautiful piano in the home, and so there's always a gathering around with everyone sometime after dinner has been served, where the sons will play and sing a few songs, and as an appropriate closing performance, Shirley would get up and bring the house down with something special. Not everybody gets to see those amazing moments, but I certainly do, viewing it from just a short distance in the background. I would have loved to see Susan Dey or Danny Bonaduce show up, not to mention other alumni of The Partridge Family, of whom the little boy who played drums, Brian Forster, is the great, great, great grandson of author Charles Dickens.

The party doesn't go on all night of course. It pretty much gets over with somewhere around 9:00 pm, so I put my 6 hours in, settle up with Marty, and we end up kicking back on the couch and having a conversation for about 15 or 20 minutes on topics other than entertainment for the most part. We became distant friends. I would call him up on the phone every once in a while and see how he was doing, and he would do the same. He's an actor too, and still does the occasional bit part on popular TV shows, but he used to arrange for celebrities to appear in TV commercials, dating way back to Orson Welles's appearances and voiceovers for Paul Masson Wines.

As is another case of Old Hollywood, I would end up seeing Shirley at The Gardenia Room a couple years ago as she came in to see a performance of a Cabaret artist friend of hers in the business. It was great to see her again, as there were a few legends in the house that night. That reminds me. I still need to finish reading the book that Shirley and Marty gave me of their autobiography titled "An Unlikely Romance". I better complete it before I give him a call. Maybe I'll send him something new from my bar product line in the mail.

The last time I bartended for them at their home, Shirley was kind enough to sign a newly-remastered DVD copy of "Oklahoma" to my mother so I could give it to her as a birthday gift. That was wonderful, as they're just a few years apart in age.

It'll be good to make contact with them again. It's been too long, and we're not getting any younger . . .

14

TRIPLE DEPRIVATION

In November of 2010, not knowing how the rest of the work/gig schedule was going to fill out for the month, some gigs had dropped into place where I knew it was going to be a marathon to cover. But as usual, I put myself through the fire. Since Sept/Oct, Lucques Catering had been trying to book me as a bartender for a couple events to get me started with them, but each initial time they made contact with a date or two, I was already booked elsewhere.

Finally we linked up with a date. It turned out to be during the annual touring weekend for MOCA (Museum of Contemporary Art) of Los Angeles, where the biggest donors are taken by bus around the city to a few routed destinations; artist's homes, galleries, and sculptor's work lofts/warehouses, to get a feel for the current works-in-progress, completed works, and future projects. Part of the perks program when you're loaded!

At the very beginning of the week, I got a call from the Patron tequila office in Santa Monica to bartend the oncoming Saturday night for a "Vegas in the Valley" casino night and silent auction/fundraiser event, with the bar sponsored by the spirit brand. The weekend was getting set after bartending at The Gardenia on Wednesday.

As the dates from Lucques were nearing, I was getting a little freaked out because I hadn't received the full gig details of info (address, call time, dress, etc.) yet from Jess. She told me via email that she works through an event planner who for some reason is paranoid about giving the details out to soon. The E.P. probably has some type of set-up where they get final payment 48 or 72 hours prior to the event to avoid the client and caterer from eliminating the middle man. You never know for sure, but you have an idea.

It makes it tough on the staff when the basic info is held back until just the day before, as you don't want an unforeseen cancellation to hit and be left without a gig when you've been strung along that far with it, possibly missing out on a party/event that came in on that same date that you said no to during the time of the gig that was booked with the no details stage of limbo/tentative/confirmed.

I didn't know what to think for a while there, not quite sure of their modus operandi at that point. I was just praying for the best result and hoping not to lose out due to something stupid and unnecessary in the first place. I had faith in Jess, though. The pay was very good, so it was going to be hit or miss!

It worked out a little better than expected, as another short gig with Lucques came on the books for the following morning that I was asked if I wanted to do also. Of course I said yes, even knowing that morning work is murder for me, as it's during my usual sleep hours. I'm a sucker for the experience and the mystery of how something's going to turn out by being there, not hearing about it later. The gig detail info finally came through.

Here I am Thursday night listening to some music and smoking a cigarette out on the sundeck in the back yard wondering how the fuck I'm going to pull this off and get some rest while wired. The confirmed scenario had me working Friday evening at the mansion of superagent Michael Ovitz in Beverly Hills on Benedict Canyon Saturday morning and early afternoon at an artist's sculpture studio/warehouse in Silverlake, and then a 5:00 pm Saturday night start with the Patron gig in Calabasas. Luckily, Calabasas is only two minutes away from where I live, right next door in Woodland Hills, so it would be a short road home at the end.

For some reason, I had a difficult time falling asleep late Thursday night. I just couldn't shut my mind off. I was resting, but could just barely fall. This didn't help matters any. I had energy Friday afternoon before the 4:30 pm call time, but I didn't feel it full power.

To avoid the 405 freeway in case of road jam, I took the 101 and got off on Van Nuys Blvd., shot over to Ventura Blvd. and went up Beverly Glen to Mulholland Drive, East past Deep Canyon and hit Benedict going back down the switchback till it leveled off and straightened out. A few minutes later I came to the event address at Leona Drive. It was then that I realized only three short blocks away was the infamous yet horrifying history of Cielo Drive. Having a few spare minutes arriving early, I made a U-turn and headed back to 10050 Cielo. This 3-acre hillside property at the end of a cul-de-sac was the scene of the infamous Manson family Sharon Tate murders in August of 1969.

Built in 1942 on land originally called "The Bedrock Properties", there was also another home on its own plateau in the distance at 10048. Together, the homes were called the "Twin House" and the "Love House". Before the ugly debacle took place during the Summer of Love, many notable stars had lived in the home previously, including Lillian Gish, Cary Grant and Dyan Cannon, Henry Fonda, George Chakiris (Bernardo in West Side Story),

Mark Lindsay of Paul Revere & the Raiders, Samantha Eggar, and Olivia Hussey.

The final resident of the original house was the musician Trent Reznor of Nine Inch Nails, who moved out a few years later explaining "there was too much history in that house for me to handle", but took the front door of the house with him when he left. In 1994 the house was demolished and replaced with a new mansion called "Villa Bella" with a new street address of 10066. The actual street and address is very close off Benedict Canyon, but the land itself is high up right off the street, deep in, and pretty much inaccessible.

Parking back on Benedict and Leona, it was time for me to head up to the event of the night. The home of Michael Ovitz is quite incredible, like four massive flats on top of each other with an impressive modern architectural design. Part of the home is an actual art museum. His garage at one side is more like a parking structure with a 25-foot high ceiling, wide open holding about a dozen cars. Being one of the first of the staff to arrive, I started separating the beverage stock for two different bars, one inside and one outside. There were about 100-150 MOCA patrons due to attend throughout the course of a 2-3 hour period, and due to the nature of the museum-part of the home they would be walking through and viewing, it ended up being a major tray-passing style of service.

Grey Goose sponsored the bars for the party, so we prepared a few specialty cocktails, as well as basic mixers, beer, wine and champagne. It was nice out, so I decided to take the outside bar set on a big balcony overlooking the South side of the property, Hollywood, and the Pacific. When you're bartending this type of top-etiquette evening, everyone working is in a little bit of a high-strung state, where the glass stemware ends up being the #1 priority of paranoia, making sure to avoid the breaking and shattering of any of this sensitive glassware when making your way through the main rooms filled with guests speaking with each other at low to medium volumes with no loud music on to overcome.

Beforehand, we were able to take a walk-through of the museum, but we had to either have the custom slippers on that they provided for all staff and attendees, or just be in your socks. Kind of a weird request, but I had done that before, though I didn't care much for it, as your feet go from wearing durable working shoes with non-slip soles to the potential of a slip-and-fall disaster on hard, polished flooring. All of this just to make sure that the floor doesn't suffer a skid mark or two? God forbid! On the tour, we were able to meet Michael. He said to the floor staff in humor "Why don't we just spill some club soda or juice now and get it over with". Funny as it seems, it's actually not a bad idea, as it kind of breaks the ice. But it was just the mention of that alone that broke some ice, so it was an understanding thought from him after he lightened it up with a laugh.

It was one of those nights again where there's an equal amount of set-up and breakdown as there was actual party time. What usually happens is the bigger the property I'm working on, the more schlepping there is to do, so you need extra hands on board to carry and load. Much the reason why I prefer working cool, smaller parties instead, but I take what's given to me with no complaints, at least not that anybody else can hear, anyway!

It goes off without a hitch. I could see the mind pressure through the eyes of the staffers falling away like beads of sweat drying back up on the skin rather than hitting the ground. I'm basically the journeyman working around and with these kids for the most part, setting them up with various cocktails to scoot off inside. I don't get rattled anymore. I just stay in the flow of things, keeping my normally high energy and responsibility paced with what needs to be done, focused and aware, yet with this gig preferring to bartend off in the distance. We fade out, finish and close, and load back up.

This is one of those places where I wished I would have brought my camera to take some quick shots while I was walking away from the home, down the long driveway to the street. I'll use it as a reminder for next time. Feeling wired from the cranking out of drinks once again, as is the usual case with all the gigs I do, I didn't know how long it was going to take before I could cool down and relax, and try to get some sleep before the early-morning rise I had to face.

Having some decent hours to crash, I couldn't fall again. The same thing happened as the previous night. I don't use an alarm because I never have to. To get up at a certain hour, I simply say the time out loud to myself, and it works every time. However, I didn't trust it this time around due to state of fatigue. I was afraid I'd sleep right through the call time, and the location was a 28-mile drive over to Silverlake. I had some power, but it felt kind of empty. I put a good breakfast in me, so that helped rejuvenate my energies for what was going to be a long day with back-to-back gigs to get through.

After grabbing a coffee/hot chocolate roadie at my local diner, Michael D's Café, I hit the 101 freeway and luckily cruised over to a few miles onto the 5 and towards the exit smoothly. All of us staffers were parked out on this small street, talking a little bit or having a quick smoke, as we were waiting for the doors of the sculptor's warehouse and offices to open so we could go in and set-up, but they arrived in short time.

As we went in the very front there was a kitchen to the right, which was very handy for the food side of the crew. The beverage product was stacked up against the wall there, so I started moving some of it over to the artist's work warehouse, eventually setting up the bar area after helping move some tables, linens, tubs and glassware with others. Everything in the large building had a clean sensibility to it, so we needed to operate the same way during service.

Some of the sculptor's work was massive in size, located mostly in the middle of the floor with other smaller pieces near the walls, so the size of the space was necessary for his craft, yet plenty of walk-around room for the MOCA patrons once they arrived for stop #2 on their day tour. The edibles provided were a tray-passed mixture of light breakfast and lunch fare well-prepared as is Lucques reputation. The bar had champagne, wines red and white, a few beers, along with bloody mary's and a few basic mixed drinks and juices.

A cool part of my job working privately and on-call is to not always have to work full bars like I have for so many years in the past. Sometimes a simpler gig is just what the doctor ordered, especially if the pay is the same. I don't always have to be behind a bar practicing mixology. Been there, am still there, done that.

The invite was expecting only about 40-50 guests in total, so it was easy for us to handle, but that was the worst thing for me at that time. I needed more activity at the bar to keep me awake. I managed fine as I'm used to being a trooper and seeing things through no matter what, but the pace of the event did nothing to help the time go by faster. Thankfully it was short and sweet, with the sculptor giving a talk and presentation in the middle of the floor during the half-way point of the exhibit. He was an Irishman in his early 40's who had put a lot of time and effort into his finished crafts. I couldn't find my way into them, though. They were a bit strange to me, to say the least. Contorted objects in wood, iron, steel and plaster, the examining of man and evolution. It was out there!

At the end of the gathering, the patrons were heading back to the bus for their next timed destination. We started fading and breaking down rental equipment and product as quick as we could, shuffling it outside to the pick-up area. It didn't take more than 30 minutes and we were done. I turned in my designated jade-colored shirt and apron to Jess, and I was on the road again.

With a few hours to spare, I headed over to the Good Earth Restaurant in Studio City for a quality lunch and a protein-powered yogurt shake called "The Surfer". That with the combination of their signature ice tea blend of herbs and cinnamon would hopefully take me on the energy drive that I needed. Upon arriving, I get a voice mail from Emily at Patron asking me if I can pick-up all the juices at the store for the cocktails I was going to be making at their Vegas event, as she was busy moving into her new digs over the weekend. It was easy for me to do, so I obliged, keeping all receipts for reimbursement.

The best thing about this event is that I was going to be busy and active from the get-go. I began to get pumped up, as much as I could make myself believe anyway, but the overall meal I had did wonders to keep me going. I headed back to the house in Woodland Hills to take a short break between gallops, change some clothing and grab my Patron shirt, listen to some rock music jams to stay in a somewhat busy mood, and eventually biking over to the Smart & Final store to raid their juice aisle, filling the backpack to the brim and then some. I dare not relax too much, for I know what would come on in a hurry. Nodding off! Couch or recliner . . . stay away!!

The Calabasas Inn has been an old staple of the area for a long time, but it had seen its better days. I backed the truck up and parked in the loading dock area in the rear of the facility, next to another vehicle. Once more, I lift my full bar kit over my shoulders, and along with the juice load double-bagged in my left hand, it felt like the weight equivalent of removing a saddle from a horse. I walk on in to get started with yet another complete bar set-up, barely getting up the steep steps to the open rear delivery door without too much sway.

A community venue for the most part, used to hosting a variety of events, had a nice, roomy and lengthy built-in bar, with an ice machine stationed back in the large kitchen. Shortly after I walked in, I got this eerie feeling about the place, like I was about to become the bartender in a long scene from "The Shining". Of course, that early evening the ice machine had to go on the blink. We salvaged a couple buckets out of it, but an event assistant had to go and grab well over a hundred pounds from the store to make it through. Glad I found out then! Had I known before, I could have grabbed them when I was at the store. I always get pissed about insignificant little things like ice and glassware being of short commodity!

I thought I'd be working with another bartender from Patron that I was initially made aware of, but was never told until I arrived that Corey wasn't able to work the gig with me. Here I was with energy depleting faster than normal, basically bar solo for the entire party. I may need a shot of something soon to keep the spirits moving within me! Keep the smile, Kyle.

The Patron product was already nicely displayed on the backbar area above the coolers, so I just had to get the recipes down and put together some pitcher batches for back stock. We had four main drinks name-based with a casino theme, a couple shaken, a couple not. It was probably best that I had a workout ahead of me. That is precisely what happened. Patron is like liquid gold to people, and when they know the bar is hosted or sponsored, than the gates of flow just open wide. This is my favorite thing about bartending private parties though, and that is, I don't have to ring anything up in a freaking cash register. It's boom, boom, boom with no transaction time stand-still. A relief of a task you can't imagine!

I'm in high gear now, cranking the drinks out like shaker rapid fire. The gaming tables are packed and running in full swing, and there was some awesome sports collectibles, guitars, and other things on auction. In whatever energy level I was in at the time, I couldn't have been happier when internal overdrive showed up to assist in matters. The engine of my body and mind were in tune to a strong RPM, just where I like it, and needed it. Before you knew it, I was well into full and fast-moving performance behind the bar, a type of physical hyper-ballet that only few can rival.

My own style is loosely tight and individually event-fitted. The video camera and interview crew gravitated over to me at the bar when they caught me guest-free in a rare moment, and we improvised a complete Patron cocktail segment "live" during the event. If you ever see it, just know that I was a quite hot wired-for-sound at that particular space of time. I haven't seen it yet myself, but it's due to be sent to me sometime soon by either link or disc.

My favorite part of the night that kept me rocking the most was listening to the music of Sam Curo, who was like a one-man band for the event. His R&B music/song selection and style was incredible, but he had this voice that sounded almost identical to Bill Withers. It was very special to hear. I could just close my eyes and it would take me back to the sound of the 70's and watching the Midnight Special. Shout out – SamCuro.com

It turned out to be a 6-7-hour haul altogether, but I made it. Fading out the bar with what was leftover to clean up, and whatever Alan the host wanted to take with him, that's when it began to slowly hit me. I was fading into a spaced-out stupor while keeping my eye on guarding the remaining bottles of the precious vitamin T that some guests thought were there for the taking after the bar closed. Not so the case, as I was trying to remain calm and pleasant during a couple toasted run-ins, explaining why they can't have as they lie through their teeth about "someone" telling them it was okay to do so. But what the bitch didn't understand is that it has to go through me. I am the gatekeeper of that shit!

After saying goodbye and thanks to Alan, I loaded the truck up for my final exit. Lighting up a cigarette in the dark dock area, I just stood there gathering my composure for a few minutes before I got behind the wheel on the rain-misted night. I was beyond tired, in that second energy phase where I'm awake and exhausted at the same time, and hungry again. That's a good sign! My drive home was less than 2 miles on back streets. What a blessing to have at the end of this journey.

Working three gigs within a 30–hour period with no sleep wasn't the way I had planned. I don't mind taking endurance to the limit, as I've had a lot of practice, but this went way over. When I finally crashed after some calm-down time at the house, I was out-of-body for 12 solid hours, pretty much missing the next day, gone by too fast for me to keep up with.

15

GIANT VILLAGE NYEve

Since the beginning of the past decade, a group of individuals have been event promoting under the name of "Giant Village". It eventually became the largest 21+over New Years Eve party in the country, right here in downtown L.A.. Initially, they started in the Westin Bonaventure Hotel on Flower Street, but slowly grew out of it over the next few years, where it flourished out onto the streets among the soaring skyscrapers on Wilshire Boulevard, the more natural environment for the letting go of as much inhibition as you can on the very last day/night of the year.

I was hired to work with Premiere Bar Catering on a few different occasions, and two of them were for this annual NYE event, in 2004 and 2006. I came close to working it in 2005, but decided to cancel out of it to work another event. 2004 marked the first time it was to be out on a square 4-street pattern (+) downtown, completely blocked off and sealed with security. This NYE fell on a Sunday/Monday so we had to wait until the police came to close the streets before the massive set-up could begin.

Mark, the owner of Premiere, rented a perfectly convenient street corner space of an empty bank as a two-night storage facility for the beverage product. He called in a bunch of us on the day before the event to come down and help unload and set-up the stock delivery from Southern Wine & Spirits and Young's Market, for the next-day issuance per bar and bartender, and for us to get a lay of the land that was going to be ours to run the following night for 12,000 ticket-paid denizens of the L.A. nightlife. When you make it through another year living in the city of angels and devils, believe me, there is good cause and reason for celebrating on the last date after 364 of them have gone by in a blink!

The palate drops of product from the trucks seemed endless. We formed a human conveyor belt from outside-to-inside the old bank quarters, finding a special behind-the-counter spot for the variety of alcohol and no-alcohol beverages, spread out and categorized by main spirits, liqueurs, beer, wine, champagne, juices, sodas/mixers, waters and fruit. The amount of overall product had equal to do with the fact that there was going to be 80-90 bartenders positioned in 20 or so bar stations blue-printed throughout both sides of the four streets, and pouring for 8 straight hours (8pm-4am), so you needed enough product to divide as fair and strategic as possible for the 20 bars and their placement volume potential, as well as having a normal amount of back stock.

With the product inventoried by Zoltan, Mark's assistant, all was in place and ready to distribute out the following day to the bartenders and their barbacks, who had the heaviest load of moving bags of ice to varied distances all night long, amongst other duties. However, I was not to be one of the many bartenders on the ground outside. Mark placed me to manage and bartend the bottle bar of a sizeable private party several floors up in a building located at a center-corner where the four streets met, that directly overlooked the party down below. I couldn't have been happier. I was lucky there was a different place to work so I could avoid a potential misplacement outside. We walked over and into the building to do a quick survey of the large empty office space to nail down where the bars would be set-up, as well as the lounging furniture, tall table tops, and other things.

On the day of, we were blessed with fairly nice weather, but a bit cloudy. Though, it was to be a bit cool out later in the night, the sheer amount of human bodies that close together over a period of time would keep the temperature acceptable and a little balmy on the ground. We parked in a structure that was set aside for staff, just a short walking distance to the center of the gig. I arrived at 4:00 pm with the long-haul mindset in knowing that I would be there on location for somewhere between 12-14 hours, so I needed to pace myself accordingly. With the various portable bars and back-tables put into place out on the streets, the bartenders were arriving and checking into their designated stations, then on into the bank to grab their beverage inventory. With my bar kit over a shoulder, I headed to the elevator of the building across the street and went up several floors to the private party space I would be managing. Besides the bottle bar I was in charge of, there was also a regular full bar placed toward the entrance of the makeshift club/lounge that housed two other bartenders, for us to collectively take care of the 200 guests expected to arrive.

With a barback assistant to help me out, we went down to the liquor storage and snagged a 4-wheel dolly to start loading up our product to wheel back over. Thankfully, it only took us a couple runs for my bar. I had a nice, easy set-up to work out of with pretty much everything I needed, including a brand-donated top cooler that eased the need of enough chilling tubs for the bottle variety of vodkas, champagne, wine and beer that I needed to keep cold all night long.

Along with the overall bar catering work that was in preparation, four entertainment stages were also being constructed at the ends of all four streets, as well as food concessions, carnival rides, fireworks, dancers, aerialists, and various theme lounges. Top-tier DJ's were flying in from all over the world, including Paul

Oakenfold, John Digweed, The Crystal Method, and Mark Farina, and there was to be a live performance from The Killers on the stage closest to where our highrise party was at. The tickets to the event were $75.

However much time was given in advance to prep-and-ready, it always goes by fast. I'm hanging out on the sidewalk for a few minutes, having a quick smoke. At this time of the year, the darkness of the sky happens quickly in the early evening. By 5:30 pm the sun is gone. The streetlights are on for almost two hours before anyone is even allowed into this huge party area. The size of it was like a visual hallucination. People are waiting at the gates in the distance, growing by the minute. All the bartenders are fine-tuning their *mise-en-place* and cleaning things up, cutting some last-second fruit, and the like. The aromas of various foods cooking were slowly permeating the air.

Before you knew it, we were rolling.

I hooked up with the promoter of the private party lounge upstairs once he arrived, letting him know everything was in place and ready to go. With promoters of this sort, you never know if they're going to pull it off or not, as they don't always tell the truth about how many tickets were actually sold. Either way, my money was guaranteed, so I just had to worry about the well-being of the other bartenders and the cocktail waitresses. As the outside started to fill up, so did we. The sound of the music was hot and thundering, as we had a DJ spinning dance music as well. It was easy to get into a happy groove within this temporary one-night atmosphere with so much energy swirling around.

It was quite a spectacle to observe. A couple times during the night I was able to go back outside to feel and hear the power of the music more clearly on the ground under the open sky, and it was cranking. It was like a scene out of the 1995 movie thriller "Strange Days", set in L.A. on the eve of the Millennium. Who knows the various drugs some people were on walking around. But if anywhere, this was the time and place for it, with nobody bothering anyone, everyone having a good time and enjoying themselves as free spirits, with security and ambulance standing by in case of emergency. Just a few minutes before midnight, everyone started getting ready to hear the roar of the crowd and the stage announcers setting the tone with timed fireworks for the turnover to the witching hour, and a new year. The DJ's were incredible, sustaining the grooves for the crowd for hours on end, and The Killers put on a killer show.

To pull off an event like this takes a lot of work and preparation in advance, with many balls in the air at the same time, and many people playing parts. Like a film, there's pre-production, shooting, and post-production. It all has to come together in a time-efficient and cost-productive way. But Giant Village had the previous years experience running it in the hotel prior, so it wasn't their first time around with it. The differences now were just the new outdoor location and the increased size, and of course the essential permits for staging the event.

After the 4:00 am outdoor ending curfew, the bars inside my club were still open to pour no-alcohol beverages all the way up until the 5:00/6:00 am legal lift to start pouring alcohol again. The promoter didn't achieve his told number of attendees, but there were plenty of people up there partying throughout the course of the night and into the day anyway. He was only off by 25% or so, which isn't a bad percentage to end up with. As the dawn came upon us, it looked like vampire weekend in there, with lilting energies walking about and lounging in couch luxury. The smoky air from tobacco and stage props created this light haze. We looked like a large group playing roles as extras in "The Hunger".

I was then replaced by a couple of Mark's longer-term bartenders at just after 5:00 am. They had come back from a break after working an outside bar, and I was on my last legs, so it was good timing. With this clever shift, I avoided having to break down my bar, as it was still open for service. Mark and his assistant were taking care of all the cash in an office space in the bank, so I grabbed my bank and bar kit, and hustled over to settle up. When you consider the 80+ bartenders each having their own bank as well, you can only imagine the pile of green that is constantly growing all through the night. If there's a negative/positive side effect to transactions of this size, it's the portable credit card machines that were used, in that you prayed they worked well and that everyone knew how to operate them without too many time-consuming glitches or screw-ups. I wasn't so great at it myself. However, for the party-goers convenience, there were ATM machines in a few places on the streets as an option.

I finished up just after 5:30 am. When it was all over outside, the breakdown of the bars and product had to be just as efficient as the set-up, which wasn't an easy thing to do considering fatigue. Hopefully the bars had very little product left to schlep back into the bank's storage area. But that was someone else's responsibility, not mine. Yet, I'm always thinking like a manager, standing out there with eyes half-shut and red behind my shades, in the middle of this bare landscape that now resembles a massive debris fallout, with a few late stragglers mixed among the rest of the staff walking the street and cleaning the bars up, collecting the trash bins, and getting rid of the remaining ice bags melting in the tubs. Overall, the event turned out and was pulled off as safe and well as one can hope for, with no fatalities.

It's a weird feeling, just standing there, empty and quiet now with the big stereo turned off, my ears still ringing from the earlier sounds while I do a visual pan of the four streets one more time before I go. I'm hungry. I'm drained. I'm spaced out like a brainless work dreg still in uniform. By a stroke of luck, I make it back to the truck without losing direction as to where the fuck it was. It helped that the parking structure was mostly empty now, which allowed me to zero in on my dark horse from afar. This is back when I still carried a joint in my ashtray for purposes of arcing my personality to relax and wire-down if necessary, but I waited and fired it up for a toke or two on the road after I figured out where the freeway entrance was to avoid being lost and paranoid behind the wheel downtown at that hour. In 35 minutes, I was home for breakfast and crash . . .

16

JUDGE AND JURY

If there's something that really rattles my cage, it's getting summoned for jury duty. The last time happened in late 2004, and previously in 2002. It's one of the calls you get that makes you feel like you're about to get hooked on a chain gang for an undetermined amount of time if selected. You receive the mail notice, make the call into the automated numbering system on the requested day, and go in when you're number is up.

Since I live in the San Fernando Valley, my location queue was the Van Nuys Courthouse, about twelve miles away from the house. Luckily, it's a convenient destination that fits many a mid-point to most bar gigs I get. This particular week, I happened to be at The Gardenia for a few week nights in a row, so I was praying this wrench in my work engine wasn't going to screw with my income.

I'm always pleading "financial hardship" to them, and though it's absolutely true, they rarely pay attention to the checkmark in that box. Although my night work doesn't completely clash with normal jury hours, it would be the equivalent of pulling double shifts for however long, case-dependent, getting paid peanuts for the day ride, and then facing another ten miles of possible turtle-paced road rage back on the 101 and into Hollywood for my bar gig during rush hour home.

There were performers at the club that I knew were going to draw good crowds, if not sold-out shows, which included dancer/singer Neile Adams (Steve McQueen's first wife) and Estelle Reiner. But I had to take a chance without calling the club to notify them of a just-in-case, trying to avoid a hasty cover by someone else. That just wouldn't be fair when you're caught between a rock and a hard place. I already had my work clothes with me to change into, and I had worked the night before the morning I ended up getting called in for court duty.

Little did I know, the cards of fate would intervene in my favor. Yet the early morning, as you may know, is hell for me to do anything productive. And getting up in the early morning after being up late from pulling a gig is a bitch. I pull through it, but not without a cost. Monday and Tuesday, I escape, but Wednesday I get nailed to the legal cross and have to go in. Van Nuys has this large waiting room for what ends up to be about 200 of us. We check in, and we all get a number to sit down with until were either called in or potentially held over to the next day, depending on the hour of the day, but doesn't always happen.

This place is such a melting pot when you look around, and here we are, the good law-abiding citizens being shaken and stirred out of our comfort zones for criminals who get to stay in theirs! Finishing my visual pan of the stable of eager participants, I notice about ten seats over in the next row facing mine is the writer/actor/voice-over artist/satirist Harry Shearer, who like the rest of us had his reading and writing materials in case of a long day of sitting ahead. Walking outside to avoid any male gawkers was the actress Christina Applegate. It's not unusual for anyone to get called in, celebs not exempt. There were probably a couple others in the bunch, but it's not much of a concern to me as it is just general curiosity.

I had brought some work with me, a new commissioned story to write for Sante magazine, which would help me from falling asleep in my chair. I get some quick chatting done with others sitting nearby, and began to concentrate on killing two with one. This is where being a writer has one of its few advantages, and great work if I take a train or a bus somewhere.

The first group of numbers gets called out for the first jury selection, and shortly after, the second. Again, I escape both. Two to three hours go by, and lunchtime soon comes around as I'm just entering the starvation mode, but it's my breakfast time. All of us break for an hour, and I jog to my truck and high-tail it over to the Lamplighter Restaurant, just down a mile or two on Van Nuys Boulevard.

Getting back, I'm thinking I may end up here all day and into tomorrow. I have to be at the club to set up the bar between 5:30 and 6:00 pm, but I may not get out of here until just before that time. I hate tight-timing issues. Nothing squeezes the sphincter more. But I'm also a completist, so loose ends and faulty closures are not my best of friends.

And then, the never-expected occurs after we're all back in our chairs in the big room. The following proves once again, that truth can be stranger than fiction.

Hearing the distant heel steps of the lady coming out of her open office door, I thought for sure she was getting ready to call out the next set of numbers for jury case #3. Instead, she asks for everyone's attention to the far front of the room. A court assistant takes over and announces to us that the murder trial of actor Robert Blake was soon set to begin. At that moment, low and behold, Blake and his attorney walk out in front of all of us, and are introduced to us onlookers.

Standing there in suits, with Baretta in handcuffs, the assistant tells us they are seeking volunteer jurors and asked any of us that wanted to participate in this special case, to come forward.

We were stunned beyond belief. It was like we were in a movie, and we were the extras! When you think of the Capote film *In Cold Blood*, this surreal time-stopping moment of melodrama was like a case of life imitating art imitating life. I can't remember anyone raising their hand, but there were probably one or two rich and retired in the group who wouldn't go bankrupt or suffer a foreclosure with sitting on a case of substantial duration and sequestering.

The last time I saw Blake was in 1990 when I served him a diet coke on the outside patio of the Westwood Playhouse during the two weeks of performances of Cabaret singer Andrea Marcovicci's *World War II* shows, and he complained about how much the soda cost. I think it was $3.00 if I recall.

I can only imagine what was on Harry Shearer's mind, certainly a script for a dramedy feature or some radio satire. Shortly after that scene had concluded, the next jury numbers get called out, and my number comes up. I was called following quite a few before me, and I ended up being in the twenties or so seated in the courtroom. The selection went by in good speed, and twelve of the first sixteen along with two alternates had been chosen. They determined that they had the jurors they wanted, and concluded the selection process.

Relief! I was free to go and get signed out with a few dollars in pay. With a couple hours to spare before heading to the club, it felt great to have that time restriction lifted knowing I wouldn't be called back in. I went to the batting cages just over on Sepulveda to crack some balls around. I was on a baseball team at the time, so I took advantage and put a little time inside the batters box, than got on the freeway to beat the traffic and psyche myself up in a work mode listening to some jamming rock for a busy night behind the bar. Getting back in the zone . . .

Update – In July of this year 2012, I worked the bar at a private gallery showing of an artist's paintings in an all decked-out backyard of one of the beautiful homes on San Vicente Boulevard in Santa Monica. Robert Blake showed up, pretty much dressed as the man in black with a cowboy hat and all. He actually looked quite good, considering he's been acting since the 40's. This time, he didn't even come to the bar, and it was hosted. A diet coke wouldn't have cost him a nickel !

17

COCKTAILS AND NOVELS

Back in 2005 I received a call with just a few days advance notice from Steve at Liquid Catering out of Chatsworth to work a bar gig at the L.A. Public Library, downtown on Fifth Street. It would be my first time to work there for an event, and was happy I had the date open to do so. I had worked several other previous gigs all around the city for Steve, mainly larger parties that required a bunch of us, so he was comfortable having me go out solo. With his bartenders, and as the owner, he just preferred to get to know you a little bit to feel confident that his service will be represented well. That's understandable. I'd do the same thing.

Chatsworth is just down the street from me a few miles, simply taking Topanga Canyon Boulevard North towards the 118 freeway. This is where my truck came in handy, as he paid me a transportation fee for hauling the bar, beverages and ice. Steve has a great set-up, as he owns a fine wine and spirits store, and has his bar service connected, so everything is right there and ready to go.

I trekked over to his shop a little early in the afternoon to give myself time to load up the inventory, and in case he had any particulars he wanted to talk over with me before I left on the road. There were a few light things that I needed to put in the front cab to avoid anything flying out on the way down. Taking the nearby 118, I decided to skip the 170 slice to the 101 through Hollywood and shift over to the 5 freeway and around to the 110. There are certain times of the day where you sense one direction over the other on the busy freeways, only hoping it turns out to be the right move.

Steve had an entrance already provided for me, where I was able to not only park on the street in front, but it was also closest to the main area where I was to set up shop for the initial meet and greet. I didn't know what the event was exactly until I got there and spoke to the person in charge. It ended up to be a reception and speaking engagement for L.A.'s true crime novelist, Michael Connelly, author of the Harry Bosch mysteries and the lawyer Mickey Haller. I was familiar with him, but had never read any of his books. This was during his book tour for what was then his latest novel "The Lincoln Lawyer", now a movie of the same title starring Matthew McConaughey, Marisa Tomei, Maggie McPherson, and Ryan Phillippe.

My job was to initially set up in a reception space provided on the lower floor for an invited guest list of about 75, serving cocktails, beer, wine, juices, sodas and waters for an hour to an hour and a half, then when they took the escalator up to the next floor's theatre seating room, as he was to speak about his book for over an hour and field some audience questions afterwards, I was to shift the entire bar and beverage upstairs to this wonderful, long reception desk close to the entrance of the room for when the event portion concluded. I would be open for drinks again nearby for the people who wanted to gather and chat with each other about the book and the author's own words during the evening's talk.

I had plenty of time to spare as I arrived downtown in pretty swift fashion, luck be the road for that day. If I would have hit some sort of periodic gridlock during the 25-mile surf, every minute counts, and you could find yourself stressing over a potential time-jam. That sucks when you do what I do, as the client is relying on me and only me, so it's best to head out early to ditch the quicksand. The one saving grace about being a night worker in L.A. is the fact that I still have my hair after all these years.

This gig was also one of those sweet, short ones, which I love to have booked in the middle of the other longer gigs in my calendar. It creates for a good mix of time duration. Having kindly thieved a 2-wheel dolly from Steve's shop to help me in my inventory-moving from the truck outside to inside, it made for a smoother move of product and the 50-pound bags of ice in tubs. The security guard directly outside the entrance door thankfully kept a close eye on the truck during my in and out.

After all was set and ready to go with beer, wine, and vodka chilling, I took a few minutes back outside standing near the truck with the driver's door open to clean up the breaking of a little sweat equity, and get my dress shirt and tie on. It's nice to have the time to clean up well and not look like you've just been schlepping cases for the previous hour. All the little nuances to take care of for a professional presence, creating a new energy as though you've just snapped your finger like Bewitched, and poof, all appeared. With all we do, preparation is the key.

I get behind the bar and finish up some quick last-minute *mise-en-place* detail and the cutting of some fresh fruit, some wines uncorked, and my Spill-Stop 285 steel pourers in place on some spirit bottles that would be of most use and request through the evening. I'm working solo tonight. It's fun in that you can create your own design and set-up for the bar top and back bar, as well as the vibe in the room from a point of over-the-bar communication with the guests. A bit different than sharing the bar space with another bartender, though either way is fine with me. I'm used to working with or without.

They started to slowly arrive. The library is a beautiful setting for this type of occasion-with-bar, as the energy in the room had a dose of tranquility about it, like most library environments do, one of those rare places in big cities where it actually feels okay to relax. It felt nice to be a part of, and the event had a cool, artistic quality to it, which always fits me perfectly.

I was in a good rhythm of pouring and talking, taking care of guests at a proper and friendly pace. I always have to keep in mind that my mood and enthusiasm for my work can dictate the right feel in a space of others attending, so it's always a good thing to keep myself in some sort of mental check. In the distance, I noticed the author had arrived to join in for some drinks and appetizers with everyone else. That was cool, as it gives the guests and friends of Michael's some initial "getting-there" time, with no hurry or interest to jockey for position upstairs.

He came to the bar and ordered a drink like any normal person, which is why I love my job, always getting a front row seat for some chit-chat with the stars of the show. I remembered what he looked like, as I had coincidentally been thumbing through a recent Los Angeles magazine that had an interview with him, so his headshot came back to mind almost instantly.

The 90-minute intro from start-to-finish went by fairly quick, and we were onto the next phase. During the last few minutes of the reception, I caught some moments to do some speedy tight-packing to make the transfer upstairs more efficient, but I had to wait until everyone had gone upstairs before I could make the actual move. Otherwise, you can look like you're rushing things, and believe me the room full of people can feel it on the periphery.

However, there was no need for me to be in a hurry. Nearby was a very handy elevator that assisted things nicely, almost too easy for a building of this size. Everything so quick and convenient? C'mon, that can't happen, can it? The reception desk at the top where I was to re-set all my needs for Part II was actually a more functional space to operate out of than the 6-foot portable I had just worked and broke down. No complaints here! All went magically into place with the perfect height of a dual countertop. I should have been taking calls and making drinks at the same time, but they had removed the phones to avoid any liquid catastrophe.

The doors remained closed to the theatre during the author's book presentation, but the restrooms were just outside those double-doors to the left, which made it irresistible proximity for the guests to not take advantage of during the course of the talk, as there was also a short 5-minute break in-between the entire session which went a bit longer than expected. During this time, I still had to stay close to the bar. As much as I wanted to wander off somewhere for a few minutes, I couldn't leave the product there unattended. And you know what happens anyway, something I call "Murphy's Bar". I could stand there behind the stick for 30 minutes and have no guests come out for a refresher, but I leave for less than 2 minutes and there will be four guests waiting at the bar for drinks when I peek my head around the corner. That shit never fails!

Finally, after some quiet and stoic patience, save the occasional customer skipping out of class for a minute to grab a quickie at the bar during the novel undertaking, they concluded and the doors opened back up for more pouring on my end. That was nice to see, people hanging out for a while longer post-speak and having another drink before heading home.

Soon I was in the middle of the final packing up for the evening, doing inventory counts, finding a place to get rid of any remaining ice and melt-water, and with the help from one of the assistants to the event coordinator (luckily he was still there at night!), I broke back down fast and furious, and out to the truck we went.

With my dress shirt back off and my sweater on, I lit a smoke, started the truck up, and drove back to Steve's shop to drop-off the remaining product and other tools of the trade. By this time, any rush-hour traffic had been gone from the freeways for close to two hours, so I was in a cruising groove back to the valley with the music on and the weather cool after a slight rain.

Another night, another gig in the city of angels . . .

18

POWER DOWN

In the late summer of 2008 I was called by an events and marketing company named Velvet Crossing, that had offices in both Las Vegas and Los Angeles, to work a gig that was to be held at the old Power Plant in Hermosa Beach. I would be working with a couple other bartending friends of mine that I had done many other private gigs with, so it made it more comfortable to say yes.

It was one of those long-trek gigs down the coast a ways that I go for on occasion, where I can leave early to get down there and kick back for a while near the water before show time. Down a little further is one of my favorite spots, Laguna Hills, where I road-tripped to a gig there for Patron tequila just a couple months prior. The waves are right there, so with a couple hours to spare before event set-up, I'd take a walk up and down the beach with my sneakers over my shoulder, then head over to this outdoor basketball half-court and into a pick-up game of 3 on 3 to get my juices going for the rest of the evening.

There was also the added benefit in an act of coincidence where I'd be meeting up with an ex-girlfriend of mine from the early 90's Denim & Diamonds days, to give her a few of my bar products to be put up as an auction/fundraiser gift. Initially, she and a friend of hers, Michelle, had made contact with me via email about the donation, and to maybe work a party for her sometime down the road. I was going to send the stuff to her, but this made it easier.

I had worked with VC before on a couple other occasions, but was used sparingly by them as it all depended on if I was open to work on a called date or not, always pending length of advance notice. The earlier booked the better. As I recall, it confirmed about two to three weeks before the actual event, which was good notice time to schedule it in, though most of the time I can have scattered dates booked months in advance, most of those for the many weddings I work each year for a few catering outfits.

The event at the plant was also an auction/fundraiser, with a guest count of about 150-200. I never thought I'd be working inside an environment and space of this nature, but that's what I like about working privately and on-call. You never know where you're going to end up next. Makes for interesting conversation! Velvet had set-up the bar's sponsors for the evening, which were Belvedere vodka and 10 Cane rum. This means that we were making some special brand drinks from those spirits of choice, along with the basic drinks, a few beers, and wines red and white.

I caught the best time in the afternoon to be on the 405 freeway from the valley over to the surf. Pulling into the parking lot after grabbing a quick bite to eat at a nearby diner, gave me time to go though my bar kit to see what I initially wanted to bring in, knowing I could always go back to the truck if I needed anything extra, that I always like to have with me for just-in-case purposes. Like I've said before, with each new gig, from a standpoint of bar set-up, you never quite know what you're walking into or what an unknown person in charge may forget to bring, but I knew with the professionalism of Scott and everyone at VC, that we would have what we needed behind the bars.

Kellie, Tami and another bartender friend of hers arrived within a matter of minutes, and they gathered at the front entrance of the facility to meet up with the coordinator, who would give a walk-through with the liquor brand reps of the layout inside where the event was to take place. I ended up taking the back receiving/delivery dock into the building, as it was closer to where I parked. I saw some people moving in and out of there, including the chosen food caterer and staff hired for the party, Outback Steakhouse, so I followed someone up the narrow steps and in.

I met up with them on the inside of the front entryway just in time for the once-over to begin. It was quick and painless, but the visual of it all was a chuckling affair. Here we were about to shake and bake cocktails in the midst of these massive curved pipes and generators that were pretty much multi-floor to ceiling. There was this low frequency hum in the air, a ghost sound of the past, like being in the engine room of the largest cruise ship afloat where the engineers had temporarily disappeared, but maybe bigger, considering the overall size of the structure and building that housed it. It was a clean interior, if not spotless, still having shine.

The bars were right in the middle of it all, where they should be. I shake my head and roll my eyes when any event bars are set-up at too far a distance away from the main gathering, as though it's an eyesore or something to have the bars in the heat of the night. That is exactly where they should be, and that is exactly where the guests prefer them, as it is always a popular mingling point, like a safe harbor.

From there we chose our bar stations to operate out of. Kellie and I teamed together at one bar with Tami and her friend doing the other bar across the way. Tami introduced Kellie and I just a couple years previous, as she thought we would get along and be a good pair with our similar experiences in LA being in the club trenches of the 80's and 90's. She was right, but her and I have more of a sibling relationship. Kellie and I are like the trusting/bonding brother and sister we never had, and we prefer it that way. We think the same and finish each other's sentences with ways of telepathy that can only be understood by twins.

I told Kellie I needed to do a fast-paced bar prep from my end to afford me enough time to sneak out of there for a half an hour to go see my ex and drop off the goods to her. Most of the time when bartenders get there that early, we don't wear our full bar dress, in case of the potential perspiration that comes from lifting, moving, and any unknown distance schlepping we may have to do in order to get everything in its place. But the brands and Velvet did a great job of having all we needed right there at the bar area, including the ice tubbed around the corner. Our job, as description consistently dictates, was to put the liquid kitchen puzzle together.

With completion of the bar in good time, I scooted out of there and into the parking lot, but went out the front entrance instead. Walking to the truck, I noticed an ambulance and two squad cars pulled up near the receiving dock in back, where I originally entered the power plant. I didn't know what to make of it and didn't inquire, as my mind was in a timed hurry to get my other business completed before the start time of the open bars.

I hadn't seen Cee Cee in close to fifteen years, so it was great to see her and to catch up a bit, though we always kept each other's contact info if necessary. She had been living down in Hermosa for some years now with her husband and two children, after moving from Brentwood. She lived only five minutes away from the plant, which was really convenient, as I had checked out Mapquest a couple nights before to make sure I wouldn't get lost on the back and forth.

Getting back to the plant, I was still in shorts and a t-shirt as it was really warm outside and on the way down for the drive, but I always bring towels, speed stick and cologne with me so I can freshen up and look new again, water lurking in a bottle in the passenger floorboard of the truck for the final hair slick attention, and a fresh handkerchief soak-damped with cool H20 for a closing facial wipe-down to heighten the senses. Ahhh . . . feels so good!

Walking in with the clean full dress requirement looking dapper and ready to roll, I noticed the ambulance and one of the squad cars leaving the property. I was genuinely curious as to what was going on since they now had been there for some time, during my 30-minute vanishing. Within just a few more minutes of me arriving behind the bar to do some last-minute detail and bar top décor, the shocking unbelievable hit us like a sucker punch to the heart that no one would ever see coming.

The event coordinator let it be known through the brand reps and the chain of staff on the floor at the time for final preps before guests arrived, that a terrible and tragic accident had happened. One of the Outback staff who was also in charge of driving the catering van where it was at that time, parked up close to the middle stretch of the decline ramp in the back delivery dock, had gotten in the van to pull it up and out of the way into a nearby parking area during the party. Standing at the lower deep end of the dock was a young female student who was working her way through college as another one of Outback's floor waiters and tray-passers for the night.

Getting the last of the large food trays arranged to take up to the makeshift kitchen area inside, she didn't see or hear it coming. The driver of the van had either let the clutch out or the emergency brake off while getting ready to start the van to move it, and may have been looking down at some paperwork or paying attention elsewhere, and didn't notice the van moving backward. The van hit the girl and pinned her up against the tall, back concrete wall that led up to the side stairs where everyone walked up and down during that time, including myself earlier while Outback was just arriving.

When the ambulance arrived, they realized she had sustained major internal injuries, but was still breathing. After getting her stabilized and into the medical unit for transport to the emergency room of the nearby hospital, we found out soon after that she had died on the way.

At the moment of hearing this end all of tragic news, with all of us on the floor shaking and stunned with disbelief, they decided to cancel the event right on the spot, feeling there was just no way to move forward and fly with this occasion. This word came down not 10 minutes before guests were going to start arriving. The timing of this fatal accident couldn't have been worse, as there was no time for any preventive measures at the moment. The valet hired outside in the circular driveway area were given notice to let soon arrivers know, as well as the coordinators notifying the guests outside when they pulled up, certainly not expecting to hear what we had all just went through.

That was it. It was over, before it had begun. We broke down the bars and product completely, but we were still in that state of mind that only allowed you to move slow at best, with reflection of how a life can be taken away from us in a moment or a snap of the fingers. There was nothing we could do. We didn't know her. Though, we may very well have met her outside on the dock earlier, helped her with something or whatever for just a second, I still didn't know who she was. We hi and bye at gigs working for different services all the time, coming together for a period of hours, and then we're gone.

I write this story for that young, innocent girl who was struck/blind-sided by a tragic momentary lapse of awareness. The food and beverage industry as a whole is disconnected to a certain level due mainly to the sheer size of it, so I also write this to all of you out there working in the field to let you now that in that late summer and early evening of 2008, we lost one of our own.

When there's a death in the hospitality family, the industry doesn't even know it or get word of it, unless of course it's some industry executive where someone pays to have it publicized in the F & B magazines, to make sure we all take a moment and recognize their contributions.

This is different. This is one of us, one of the unsung heroes on the floor as a front house staffer. We didn't know her, but that doesn't matter. We feel for the loss of her. We feel for her family's loss of her. We feel for the other co-worker who may now be living with a lifetime of grief and regret for the accidental causation of this terrible tragedy. We pray for our great industry loss on that day, and for everyone there on location, where we were all a team for a moment in time.

This is a shout-out to the industry about the loss of this girl's life, a life just as important as anyone else's.

19

OSCAR NIGHT AT MR. CHOW

It was around the third week of February, 2009. I had been in the middle of a slew of bar gigs, something like ten in twelve days in a variety of venues and some private parties. I knew at the end of this stretch I was going to need a couple days off in a row to recuperate my slowly disappearing energy. Those precious days off would come at the very end of this close to two-week gig run.

I was aware the tail-end Sunday event was coming, as it had been in my gig schedule for a few weeks in advance, fitting in perfectly with the rest of them. I love it when gigs line up nice on the calendar, where you get lucky in reducing the risk of losing out on any gigs that could double-book on the same date. When you work on-call as much as I do, you're hoping that not everything coming in is clashing just on weekends. With a big city like Los Angeles, there are events of some sort going on during the weekdays too, so with that and filling the rest out at The Gardenia, I'm able to pull it off as pretty regular work. Otherwise, it just wouldn't be enough to make it happen.

Patron tequila were sponsoring the bars at the after-party for the Academy Awards at the famous restaurant, Mr. Chow, in Beverly Hills. The event was called "A Night to Make a Difference", hosted by the Leeza Gibbons Memory Foundation and Olivia Newton-John's Cancer and Wellness Centre. As you can imagine, there were a ton of stars showing up for the party, and the musical director for the performers on stage later that night was none other than David Foster.

I had travelled over the hill from the valley to get there a little early because those streets in and around Rodeo Drive are a bit narrow and can get congested at anytime. My goal was to get to a certain parking structure that fell alley-side to the back of the restaurant behind Camden Drive, and if you miss a side street than it becomes this U-turn scenario until you can locate the main entrance, which of course was not off one of the main drags.

I arrive and park up on the third tier. Locating the elevator after getting out of the truck, I took a couple minutes and walked over to the edge where I could overlook across the way and see the tent they had put up in back of the Mr. Chow property. It was cloudy that day with a chance of rain, so it was a good thing they did. I walk in and meet up with Emily to get the skinny on the set-up. Out of all the gigs, this last one was going to be the longest of the bunch, some 12 hours.

It was an inside/outside event, which couldn't have been better for this big-time gathering. Inside the restaurant was pretty tight even during our thankfully long set-up period. There's cameramen and staging people moving everywhere, not to mention all the floor staff and security. We had three bars in and three outside to put together. From the main product storage area out in the tent, I had to delegate who was going to get what and how much. When you're dealing with the spirit of Patron popularity, I find myself always keeping an eye out to avoid the goldmine getting taken advantage of. I have respect for the brands, and in working with them, I want them to know that I've got their back. Anytime I carry a case of Patron over my shoulders, I can feel the eyes following me.

We had a half-dozen or more bartenders that had never worked with us before, so I had to quickly give them the run-down with the product coverage and special drink recipes for the evening, having faith they would know how to do their thing with minimum or no further interference from me. The last thing I want is to have to worry about anyone doing their job professionally. Once they adhered to the understanding that they would be representing Patron as a brand bar sponsor, I knew I could count on them to keep it in gear.

Corey was a young bartender that had recently been hired as one of Patron's on-call staff, and he was going to be working alongside me behind the main 12-foot ice bar created by Carving Ice out of Anaheim. I've known Roland and Dan of Carving for years. In 2004 I shot a video segment at their facility for the Liquid Kitchen show I was co-producing with a friend of mine. We ended up in the freezer with Roland as he was finishing up the carving of the Spiderman 2 ice bar to be taken that day to set-up on the Santa Monica Pier for the film's release party.

With the dishing out of inventory to the bars and bartenders in their places, I soon got out of their way so I could do my own prep. As I slowly walked over to my station, the Carving staff was soon to complete the main bar base and flooring for the monster ice sculpture with dual luges. I get to the back tables to stay out of their way a little longer, and Corey and I pull the *mise en place* in line according to our individual and collective needs and expectations. The 50 lb. ice bags were dropped off at the bars in good time so we could start chilling some things.

For those of you who don't know, a luge is a funnel-like twist & turn tubing that's frozen in a sculpture placed on the bar top for pouring through. It has an actual funnel at the very top entrance, and ends with the liquid falling into a martini glass at the bottom, by carving a usually square space for the glass to slide in and out as an entertaining way of service for the guests. They love it! I shake the drink and then let them know it's coming down. My focus is to pour just enough to avoid splashy overfill. You get good at it after awhile, as long as you can pour and view the levels at the same time. Carving's gallery is at CarvingIce.com

There were some sandwiches being passed around for the staff during preparation, so I grabbed one knowing it would be long hours before I could actually sit down and have a real meal. We had some break time left over, so I walked back into the alley and scarfed with a few others. I walked back up to the truck and took a few minutes to wipe down and change into my shirt, have a smoke, and re-gear my mind from prep to greet-and-pour mode. Getting back, Emily brought over a duffle bag of Patron goodies for me to guest-distribute as I saw fit during the night. The first thing I had to do after peaking inside was find a good place to hide it underneath. Even that is highly-desired merch. Since we don't have enough of this material for everyone, I have to be a bit selective in issue.

I started chatting with the two main cameramen who were going to be shooting outside, and in knowing the couple shoulder-camera guys that I noticed were going to be roaming in and out, I asked the two mains if they wanted to wear Patron shirts for the evening. They were totally stoked about it, and I was happy to have a size that fit them pretty well. I figured at some point in time, those two were going to have cameras pointed back on them for a quick shot and pan, so it was a quality move.

I can't tell you how many celebs, producers, and whoever else was on the guest list, so I'll just lay out who I do know was there: Forest Whitaker, Jane Seymour, Paris Hilton, Slash and Perla, Michael Buble, Rodney Peete and Holly Robinson, Tony Hawk, Jessica Biel, Suzanne Summers, Teri Hatcher, Alan Thicke, Brooke Burns, Dr. Phil, Larry King supposedly, Terrell Owens, Eva LaRue, Deidre Hall, Mario Lopez, Fran Drescher, Thelma Houston,

Melissa Gilbert, Erin Gray, Amy Smart, Marla Maples, and of course, Leeza, Olivia, David, and Mr. Chow himself.

Also attending were John Paul DeJoria and wife Eloise, along with a table of Patron executives and some of JP's daughter's racing team. Upstairs inside the restaurant, they had a VIP Touch-Up Lounge with celebrity hairstylist, Ken Paves, sponsored by Aveeno. This post-Oscar event was special in that it was also going to be an interactive viewing party and webcast. The whole place was going to be live.

The weather was not bad, a little scattered rain, but it was just a tad on the humid side, especially in the tent, so the heaters had to be monitored so the temperature would be nice, as it gets warm with more and more bodies that eventually fill out the area. The corner wings of the tent opened up to also manage fresh air moving in for balance whenever needed.

It was underway. Party time! They had the Paparazzi, News, and Entertainment Television cameras set up for the grand entrance as guests started arriving. From start to finish, it's quite a big responsibility to coordinate. My hat went off to everyone involved. With six bars for about 300-400 guests coming and going, we handled it fairly easy, but the inside bars would get hit first, so both Emily and I were checking in here and there. Then it becomes our turn behind the bar to perform in front of the cameras outside. The ice bars were a hit as always, guests gravitating over to the lighted and slowly melting artwork, and we had a great time through the night making drinks, enjoying the atmosphere, and sharing some laughs.

When I'm working ice bars, I'm always wondering how long they're going to last before areas of the bar start to separate, crack, and cave. You can always count on 5-6 hours, but depending on how thick the main bar is vs. outdoor/indoor temperature will determine how long it will survive beyond the norm. This is another reason why I didn't want it to get too warm in the tent too fast. The degrees had to be right for everything involved. The miracle and high-five of the night, behind the scenes anyway, was that the ice bar broke a previous record and lasted 10 hours before any risk came into play. Roland and Dan couldn't believe it, but were very happy.

There were performances on stage by Olivia, David, Two Spot Gobi, an impromptu performance by Michael Buble, and a set by the young but incredible voice of Philippine singer, Charice. I think most of it is on YouTube. David Foster was certainly enjoying himself after a few drinks, getting up on stage and talking with the audience, and accompanying performers on piano. The stage was about 25 feet away to the right of us. Corey and I had a great view of the entire tent area as we stood on a platform that lifted us up close to a foot. Observing and pouring!

All those hours, though. I had to have a couple drinks myself to keep the energetic groove on to the end. The steady flow of guests at the bar during the course of the evening helped a great deal to avoid feeling a sense of fade. Once that hits, it's hard to recover, depending on how many back-to-backs you've already done in the nights before. I know what sports athletes feel when the second half of their game is not quite the same as the first half. You become a machine, grinding it out and getting through it till time expires and you can go hit the showers.

Then at the end, you have to breakdown everything and guard the remaining bottles of liquor with your life, before the vehicle-loading takes place. I new the long bar to the left side in the tent with four of the new bartenders was going to need some watching from a distance after their hours were up, as they took off before us. But one can only do so much at that hour with many liquored lingerers licking their chops for a bottle of the precious. Things can make it through the net if you look away for even 10 seconds. But ultimately, I am not the Patron Police. Therefore, not entirely responsible, not with six bars anyway. You cover what you can.

I was there from 2:00pm to 2:00am. By the time I headed back up to the parking structure with bar kit in tow, I was seriously dragging, but doing my best to hide it until I was in the elevator up and away from anyone, preferring to choose my point of collapse a little more carefully. It was such a relief to complete the stretch of gigs, but I was starting to get that thing in your throat that silently tells you that catching a cold is near.

Food and rest was the only thing left I had the energy to think of, except for maintaining open eyes on the drive home. I was a bit wired though, so that helped. My usual once-a–week tincture pop of Echinacea and Goldenseal keeps my immune system powered up 99% of the time to keep healthy, but I was feeling run down. The next day and the day after, it came on. I was out of commission. Perfect timing for my days off, though, but I would have much rather not burned the midnight oil to the point of no return.

20

INTEL

Parts I and II

__Part I__

Soon after I got out of Lakeside in 2002, I was hustling the energy to create a full solo on-call working situation, freeing myself from 20 years of doing just the opposite. I needed a change in how I went about utilizing my resume, as L.A. is not a town where experience matters. Age discrimination runs rampant with the help wanted wording, interviewing, and asking for headshots and gender. They slide by with evasion loopholes that do just enough to cover their asses. They don't care.

The managers and owners here ask for experience and knowledge, but hire youth and image. The glorified model-like high-end version of hiring titties for taverns! But that's pretty much most of L.A. in a nutshell, although I hope it's changed a little for the better over the years. Half the time if not more, the interview process can slowly become a mild exercise in sucking up, all depending on the degree of get-along and similar wavelengths with both understanding what's needed. Otherwise, an insult to one's experience, and an embarrassing gauge of inaccuracy of a person's capabilities can occur, especially if the conducting interviewee has less experience or a different position than who they're hiring. Then it becomes a battle uphill to secure fair ground, aside from the fact that when it comes to bartenders, action and production of service behind the bar always speaks louder than words.

I don't have a problem with it as much as I just wish they'd learn how to hire a preferred combination of both experienced and inexperienced, blending the two for optimum floor fusion and for educational/training purposes. L.A. for the most part is still a bit dysfunctional in the important areas such as future industry progress. The city the NRA wants to stay away from. This is why L.A. has the hardest time getting its hiring shit together, lagging behind for superficial reasoning, with no set of standards or minimums in place to insure the risk of smooth running.

Currently, however, there is a new organization in town and in eight states throughout the country called the Restaurant Opportunities Center of Los Angeles. Their mission is dedicated to winning improved conditions for restaurant workers everywhere. It's a good re-start, and hopefully they'll succeed with many of their positive actions for us all.

There I was, the whole package, a four-tool player; youth, image, experience and knowledge. I mean, Christ, I was like a modern day version of Dorian Gray but without the dark side, at that time anyway! Middle managers (are there any of those left?) can be intimidated by the experience of others. You can feel it when the air of silence and fear between the word exchange gets heavier and slower of pace. They'll never admit it of course, and so we both lose out. The best managers to work with are the ones where it doesn't have to be their ideas to implement. Improvements can get done quicker. And they're the ones preaching teamwork!

I don't want their jobs of 50-hour misery. Been there, done that, more than once, no longer interested, thank you very much, now read between the lines and understand I want to work the bar and nothing else! Get it, good!! However, I fault myself back then to ignore when the ad says minimum of 1-2 years experience, of which most of them post like bad standard practice. It pretty much tells you the experience level of the people in charge, who for the most part really did nothing more than just grab a job themselves. These ads also use those all-telling hype words like "Dynamic", "Energetic", "Career-Minded", and "Team Player", but you can only prove those attributes in action, when you turn the switch on. Otherwise, it's like a clown jumping through hoops of fire in a small, cluttered interview office, you know, where the imposters succeed, and then fail on the floor. No thanks, I'll pass. There are some places where it may just be better to avoid working in.

Imagine if the ad requested a minimum of 10 years experience. This would help alleviate the filtering to the bottom, and would actually pull a bar group of substantial, collective intelligence together in one house, like a sports team. A combination of players who have the experience and knowledge to spread out the floor, that also provides a depth of stimulation with something to say. Customers of all ages have a proven appreciation for that. But managers have a tendency to shoot high and aim low, choosing the narrow and unproven road many times over the wider scope of vision, where they may fear some loss of control. They'll play it to their version of safe and in charge by just hiring the desperate youth for the most part, who have far less experience to offer. All in all, it's better to have the right mix of individuals behind the bar, having newcomers learn from the advanced bar men and women of Food & Bev.

Tenure works for you only once in a while, either through a connection in, or when you luckily run into an individual with that rare quality and respectable insight into a person's best interests at heart for the establishment. L.A. is big and spread out, so that adds to fewer people knowing each other from various places of work. Sometimes the excuse of over-qualification can rear its ugly head, but in my opinion, there's no such thing as being over-qualified when it comes to working behind the bar. Not today, not ever.

The problem with my resume is not padding it, it's reducing it down to an acceptable level to be seen, called in, or considered. There's no possible way I could put close to 30 years of bar experience on a one or two-pager. It would have to be a minimum of 3 pages. But then, that becomes intimidating to some. Only in our industry does more experience equate to less work, so be careful how much you gain, as you may have to hide some of it depending on the seeking venue. I'm just not revealing everything, not if it doesn't work in my favor. I have to pick and choose while doing the best I can to get a feel for them. Are they open to someone with my level of work history? Should I keep my published works in the industry magazines off the resume? How do I get the job without losing the job from innocently intimidating the chiefs? The endless chess moves for employment. That's all we need, a layer of grief on top of the stress cake!

Though the industry could use a restructuring of its hiring and filtering practices to acquire the best staff possible, it'll never happen. Hospitality is just too big, therefore fractioned to the core. And with the association's lobbying powers in Washington to keep things the same and greater unity away as they side with the owner's preferences to keep cheap and pay $2 or $3 an hour to tipped floor staff in Colorado and a few other states and/or establishments that enforce it with ruthless abandon. We are so thankful for your care and concern for the well-being of your own!

If ever there was an industry in need of a Dexter to clean up all the wrong doings, screw-jobs, the mass of unfair practices, life and economic ruining, and to straighten out the never-ending mecca of fucked-up, cocaine and ego-driven ownership and management that gravitated here to the land of make-believe, it's Food and Beverage. I promise, if you let me shape-shift into this dark-of-night Mad Hatter character, I'll do my best to complete the necessary and way overdue repairs in one season . . . . . or two if it's fun! The end problem is that many of us would like to have a career-like profession in Hospitality, but keeping employed in this industry is too unstable and insecure with many establishments coming and going.

So I moved on from all those years of soil and toil, temporary stabilities, and living with uncertainties. Everybody faces it in this business if you're in it long enough, but you grow tired of it. It wasn't easy leaving Lakeside, as it was a beautiful property and club with a great bunch of members, and I was taken good care of while employed there. But each year, they seemed to be slowly reducing events and activities, and it got to a point where the energy of the club started to dissipate from the busy environment we were used to. The shift schedule reduced a little, and with the other bartenders having been there with many years of seniority, there was nowhere to move up. It became time to go. On the last night there, I closed up the bar close to 11:00pm, with a few members still playing poker in the card room, and walked out into the mist of the November rain and the lighted darkness of the near-empty parking lot, waved goodbye to the guard at the security gate, and never returned.

To this day though, I still talk with my executive chef friend who was at the club during that time, who's moved on to a GM position at a Marriot property down in the Newport Beach area, as well as chatting with the Lakeside GM from the same time, and of course, bartender Bruce Heighley. In fact, for a few years after, I even bartended private parties at some of the member's homes. Though the change in the activity level at the club is true, something strange happened there that coupled with my departure, but I promised not to speak about it. It's been 10 years, no sense in cracking now.

Part II

My solo work started to grow pretty well, and I gained more contacts with almost every gig. If you do good work and show your professionalism with service, it usually leads to getting more. I have my business cards and pens to make sure they don't forget. Most people in L.A. don't operate with the best long-term memory, so one must permeate like an alien virus, but in a good way. I was also back on full-time availability with Tabi at Tender Bartenders, whose service is the longest-running in town, some 30 years now or more, where she has these old, classic clients. I also went back on regular call at the Hollywood Palladium and The Gardenia.

Soon into 2003, I got hooked up with a man named George at the Encino Banquet and Gardens for more on-call work. However, this property was primarily St. Mary's Parish, an Assyrian church located on Lindley Avenue in the Reseda/Tarzana area, just a few miles down the 101 from where I live. Always a good find! George was the Pastor/Bishop there, but I also dealt with him when it came to booking me on the bar for a variety of events. The banquet room and gardens are located in the back half of the property, not visible to the street, but not hiding either. It's an advertised venue. He has the whole shebang there, a huge event space that holds 300, good portable bars, an ice machine in the kitchen, and a liquor cage to house what the client buys. In this new position I was now creating for myself, I realized that hustling and hunting go along with the job description, building a good reputation along the way, and branching out wherever I could.

One day I get a message from George to work a wedding and reception, and that he has a caterer coming in who needs an extra bartender. For the first time I was introduced to Bobby, the owner of Bahador, a Persian catering company out of Tarzana as well. After a busy night with the bars under control and flow, he asked for my card. This was beginning to work. I was soon booking gigs with him a little more regularly, filling in any open dates, but I not only had to teach him to call me with as much advance notice as possible, due to bookings from other outfits, but had to bring him up to speed with my bar knowledge from an operational standpoint, so he would have what I needed product-wise behind the bar, aside from the big bar kit that I bring in with me. He had to understand how to make the bar an initial source of focus and placement at parties, instead of it being shoved over in a corner or off the beaten path somewhere, not easily seen. People want to know where the bar is, and they want it convenient. His primary thing was food, so I understood where he was at.

I still had my long hair at that time, which he thought had some unique quality to it when it came to working his private events within the Persian community in the valley and in Beverly Hills. It was only another year or so when after many years of having the mane, I finally cut it all off. Thinking of just a partial trim at first, I gave way so I could gather the more than a foot of strands in a large Ziploc and send it to Locks of Love in Florida for cancer patients, which was my second time in doing so. It has to be 10 inches or longer, or they don't accept it. At one of his gigs I'm on later in the week, I came in through the side gate of the house. I didn't tell him about the barber encounter. He's in the house, and I'm setting up the bar outside. I have a hat and sunglasses on, semi-disguised. About half an hour later he walks out of the house with some back stock product for the bar, and almost drops the case in shock. He said "Kyle, is that you? What happened? Why did you cut your hair . . . you lost your power!" I started laughing. He says "No, really, your hair was your power". I said "Yes, I know, but it was time for a change. I'll grow it back sometime again". There is a truth to what he said, but you only notice it when you have it really long and then cut it down to just an inch or two.

I also felt at the time that the hair image in L.A. was changing again, back to a shorter look and preference, whether it be a clean look and shave, or the semi-mod shadow and mess o'hair look of today's generation, a slight difference from the British mod look of the late 70's/early 80's. Again, with so many different types of

123

venues and outfits available to work out of, it was best to stay somewhat within the overall visual groom image of approval. Even I conform once in a while!

Sometime after I made the cut to short and easy, I noticed a change in how some of the Persian men were treating me. I had always gotten along well with the women. The women have a beauty about them that is staggering. They're the jewels of the Middle East. But the guys seemed to be looking at me with a question mark, yet nice with communication. Some would stare, look back to their friends and chat, and so on. I could see it peripherally, and became curious myself. I had felt this feeling before. Was it my demeanor? Then, a memory dawned on me.

When I was hired in 94' at Café Bellissimo near where I live, I was invited to one of the owner's birthday party/dinner before the night of business at the restaurant got going. This was a Sicilian-owned establishment, so when I arrived from walking across the boulevard, both Tony and Emilio looked me over for some seconds. I was still fairly new and hadn't quite got to know everyone yet. Greetings and some light chat ensued, and it came down to the owner-brothers wondering if I was wired, carrying and working undercover for some level of law enforcement/secret service, as it was mentioned with only half-humor. Comically bewildered, I let them know I was clean and not who they thought I might have been. Hard to remain normal at that point, but I did my best to fit in with everyone else, though it took a while for the surprise to leave my face. I ended up working with them for five years, trust gained. Emilio didn't like me too much, though I gave him no reason for it. It's just one of those things you can't do much about, so I kept my distance to avoid tangle, his wife Kelly kept me on, and Tony moved me over with him when he opened up the Thousand Oaks restaurant.

A little note of interest – Emilio Bellissimo was also Tony Valentino, the lead guitarist of the 60's L.A. punk garage band, The Standells. Their smash hit "Dirty Water" in 1966 went to #11 on the charts. The original members got together and performed at Game 2 of the World Series at Fenway Park in 2004. The original organist for the band, Larry Tamblyn, his brother, the actor Russ Tamblyn, played the role of Riff, the gang leader of the streetwise Jets in the musical film of West Side Story. Russ was discovered at the age of 10 by Lloyd Bridges. Russ' daughter is the actress, Amber Tamblyn. Today, I believe Emilio still lives right down the street from me, literally, about 20 houses down. I think he's pretty much retired now. If you delve into Hollywood and L.A. enough, you'll see a small world of a 100-year string of people who know or knew each other.

Cafe Bellissimo was a pair of singing-server restaurants. The only other one in town was Miceli's in Studio City. I'm sure with Emilio and Tony's musical backgrounds, it was a good way to get the surrounding valley community together and discover some great new talent, of which they did very well over the years. It's always nice to give back!

Though, three years in when I was at Tony's Café B in Thousand Oaks, something similar happened. An older guy started coming in during late afternoons for some wine and a small bite at the bar. He was one of those occasional regulars. As we talked several times over a stretch of months, and even in depth when time allowed before the main rush, he let me know he was retired CIA. I started asking him questions about his field of work out of curiosity. His responses weren't always direct with the questions, but he answered safely enough. He did let me know that Thousand Oaks was home to the most retired high-level law enforcement officials in the country, guessing CIA/FBI, along with the most retired Mafia/Mob bosses. Either they never stop watching each other, or they're in cahoots. I thought that was an interesting piece of information, but found it an almost impossible stat to verify as well. At another time, he let me know that if I ever wanted to consider going to work, I would have to learn three specific languages. One of them was Gaelic, but can't remember the other two, though I probably have them written down in some pile of notes from the past.

The Persian Men were doing the same thing to me, but a bit more subtle. Over the course of the five years where I was working many gigs in the community, there was the occasional verbal inquiry at the bar in regards to some thinking I was working undercover there too. I guess I just have this look and disposition about me that steers them in that direction of thought. I still work gigs for them today here and there, but not through Bobby, as I heard something happened between him and his tribe, and they've been on the outs for a few years now, with catering. Either that or he faked me out and is using someone else besides me. Most of them are Iranian, but the Armenians and Israeli's like me to work their parties too, though I end up getting the same watchful eyes at times. They're all different experiences, and I always win as long as I can prove myself, building trust over a length of time.

Persians know how to throw a party. They don't mess around. I enjoy a good time with them. They have their bands or DJ's, and they do their traditional dancing and singing. It's wonderful to see. Funny, even though they're rich and have these amazing homes all over Beverly Hills, they still try to price down gig/service fees like they're buying goods at a flea market. They're super nice people, but I guess some things never change no matter where you live. It just doesn't fit their wealth, and would look much better on them if they adjusted our American paying and tipping custom into their dealings. But to penny-pinch with human/guest services while they spend $10,000 and more on floral decor for one night is a bit out of balance. Like I've heard several say, "they spend it on themselves, not anyone else". You get to watch some of them become these image queens and kings, and that's all that matters, outdoing each other party to party. They enjoy each other and have a good time too, like all partygoers, and beyond it all, my job at these many events is simply what it is as well. No more, no less.

Bobby told me a long time ago that Persian Muslims will tip, but Persian Jews do not, so I made sure to set my fees accordingly, not relying on either! With this simple method of set-up, it really doesn't matter where I work. I can get along with everyone. With certain private parties depending on the occasion, I prefer the straight-up fee with no bar-top tipping, no jar. It just takes the issue off the table, and many times it's to the client's preference to tip at the end. The good thing is many of their get-togethers also fall on weeknights, as they party by their own tradition and holidays. I'll take the gig and move on with no complaints, as I make different monies at various venues and outfits of work anyway, so it's always changing.

They prefer good American bartenders, male or female, working their many parties, while at the same time some of their big business people of the community wonder if I'm straight up with them, or if I'm pulling double-duty undercover. The last time I was confronted at the bar was a New Years Eve party a few years ago, up in the hills off of Sunset Boulevard. With my clean look, I must be the perfect type in their eyes who could pull off such a thing, and long-term. Three of them approached the bar and said "Are you sure you're not working undercover?" Another says "You look like you could be working undercover for, you know, as CIA or FBI agent or something!" Again, I chuckle and say "No, I don't do that sort of thing. I've been working LA bars for years. What makes you think that?" They said "You just have this whole thing about you that makes us wonder. But we like you, you're very good". I must look too professional when I get it done behind the bar for them. Maybe it looks a little too good, like a form of department-trained over-compensation.

When they mention that sort of risky inquiry, though, it can make them look just as suspicious, like they have something to hide, always looking over their shoulder like there in some espionage thriller, curious if an agent/operative of big brother is watching from the bar, and I'm the spy! It must be the way of the world in the Middle East, where anyone in any position is capable of gathering intelligence. These parties are also part-in-place of how they go about conducting business in corner areas where they can't be heard, as well as in the middle of the loud Persian music that goes on for hours. However, I would have to know their language of *Farsi* in order to pick up on anything, and I would have to be wired for sound on top of it all. Luckily, I've never been frisked yet! Pretty ballsy of them though, to put me on the stand right before the party started. Then again, what if I was?

This thought brings Lakeside back once more for an encore, where I used to serve drinks to the L.A. head of the FBI for the years I was there. That time was just before I went into freelance, working privately on-call. Now that I think about it, I hope it wasn't the reason why Bobby fell out of catering popularity with his own people. However, I've talked with him on the phone a few times in the last couple years. It's always good to catch up. Bobby is a really good guy. But most of his catering has always been through the big hotels, which is how he started up. Always busy, always hustling, at a point I think he may have just ran into a case of over-extend with his catering company, trying to handle all that was coming in, because the money is right there on the table. Who wouldn't do the same? Things can fall through the cracks and quality can suffer a little bit. I remember a couple times where he probably hadn't slept for a few days.

Such is life in big city food and beverage . . . and other things !

21

EQUINE

Still living in the Burbank area at the time, I was working the lobby bar and as a banquet bartender at the 4-Star Registry Hotel at Universal City, a union property, right next door to The Sheraton Hotel, both up on the hill, walking distance to Universal Studios. This was around 88'-90'. Close by, I also found myself picking up extra bar work at the Los Angeles Equestrian Center over on Riverside Drive, located across the 134 freeway from the famous Forest Lawn Cemetery/Memorial Park, close to Griffith Park.

The center is a beautiful 75-acre multi-use everyday facility, housing 500 boarding stalls, the Equidome show arena that seats 3,500, exhibition rings, hunt and cricket fields, banquet and ballrooms, restaurant and bar, polo room, offices and more. I would work all bar areas for them on-call, as they held regular events of all kinds throughout the year for many of their members and supporters, as well as booking parties, weddings, and company gatherings as an in-house caterer to the general public. A lot of wealth hung out here, as well as many celebrities who owned horses and enjoyed the community and lifestyle.

One time before I even started to work gigs there, I got off work at Bombay Bicycle Club one night and headed over to the arena. The actor, Rutger Hauer, was putting on a short riding show with his own Friesian Stallion, the same Netherlands breed of the black beauty he rode in the 1985 movie *Ladyhawke*. Originally thought to be his own horse in the film, Othello was actually a circus performer owned by Manuela Beeloo. I was lucky enough to sneak back to the stable to meet and chat with him for a couple minutes, after he finished, as he is one of my favorite actors, especially after seeing *Blade Runner* about a dozen times over the years. I couldn't pass up the chance with this international film star. I knew it would be a once-in-a-lifetime encounter.

He was a big dude, quiet and kind, but powerful. I had only been in L.A. for a few years at that time, and though I had met and served several celebs in the area, the star-struck thing hadn't wore off that much yet, and I had strong jitters being in Rutger's presence. I didn't want to come off being young and dumb hanging with him for too long, so after talking about his horse and movies with him, I exited my foolish heart before I said something stupid, too intimidated to use my camera for a picture, and no one else around to take it. After meeting him, the snapshot idea kind of dissolved of interest. I was trying to act a little more mature than I was. I regret that now. It would have been better just to remain the shy, inquisitive kid I've always been.

I worked many parties and wedding receptions at the center, as well as the main bar and restaurant over the course of a couple years when they called me in. But if a bar manager ever departed, with me not always on the regular staff schedule, I needed to hear about it in quick time to go back in and greet the new department head, so they wouldn't forget or overlook me for the on-call schedule. This happened one time while employed. There's always something to watch out for. The organized chaos never ends in larger establishments.

Another very special time, I was called in to bartend in a private room for Willie Shoemaker's 58th Birthday. It was a short get-together of 30-40 guests over a 2-3 hour period. Eventually, after others arrived to celebrate, Willie, the racing legend and 4-time Kentucky Derby Winner, walked through the door, accompanied by his gorgeous blonde wife, Cindy. This was right around the time when he announced his retirement. I had never seen a jockey up-close before. No wonder the horses kick ass. They feel almost nothing in the saddle! Willie was 4'11" with a 96 lb. riding weight.

Following the greetings with some of his friends, he came up to the bar and ordered a Johnnie Walker Red on-the-rocks. 23 years later, I still remember. He asked my name, we shook hands, and he asked how I was doing. He was very nice and cordial, simple and normal to chat with. I poured him his drink, and told him it was an honor to meet him, and we chatted about the grounds of the L.A.E.C. for maybe 20 seconds. I couldn't ask for more. Those seconds felt longer, though. I had the utmost respect for his incredible accomplishments over 40 years, a bit in awe. Though short in stature, he was a giant in his field, the greatest jockey of the 20th century.

It was so unfortunate that just a few years later in 1991, he ended up in that terrible accident that left him paralyzed from the neck down, when he lost control of his Ford Bronco while trying to call home on his cellular phone, going off the road and down a 50-foot embankment out in San Dimas, California. Willie passed away of natural causes in 2003 at the age of 72.

The Polo season usually goes from April to October. I had never even seen a polo match before, and at that time didn't know that the center actually had a team. They were called the L.A. Stars. They didn't play on the traditional 10-acre grass field. Instead, they competed in the somewhat smaller area, though sizeable, of the Equidome riding arena. This sport has been around a long time, dating way back. The bar manager calls to schedule a few work dates with me, and I start to bartend in the arena during the weekly polo matches, or bi-weekly depending on the home/away schedule, and other events at the same time. This was interesting. I'd set up the portable bar in the middle of one of the long side walkways just in front of the stands, and there would be another bartender on the other side of the arena in the same position. We had plenty of space to work with, but it was right out in the open.

I remember waiting on the late, great character actor, Richard Farnsworth, an Academy-award nominee for best supporting actor in 1978's *Comes a Horseman*, best actor nominee for 1999's *The Straight Story*, as well as other notable films including *The Grey Fox*, *The Natural*, *The Two Jakes*, *Misery*, *Anne of Green Gables*, *Havana*, and dozens more. Originally, he was a stuntman, and co-founded the Stuntmen's Association in 1961. He doubled for Kirk Douglas, Steve McQueen, Henry Fonda, Montgomery Clift, and Roy Rogers to name a few. Yes, I do remember, he had a glass of chardonnay! There was also Dick Smothers who came to the bar, and Sylvester Stallone had his own VIP seats.

It was during this time where mixed emotions started to creep into my consciousness while bartending these matches. After watching the movement of this basically simple sport in order to understand more and more about the rules, time periods of play, and so forth, it became my opinion that it was the most ridiculous team competition that I've ever witnessed, guys on horses with a long mallet stick leaning left and right over the side of the horse chasing and hitting a ball on the ground until it goes into a goal. One of the players on "our" team was the husband of the 70's/80's country pop star Juice Newton. Remember her hit single "Queen of Hearts"?

It's one thing to see humans beat each other in competition. This is just our current state of evolution, which most certainly isn't ascending at the preferred pace of the universe, I'm sure. But with this sport, it's the polo ponies doing all the work, exerting the most energy, and put in the middle of the highest risk, without knowing or caring who the hell is winning or losing. You see the constant jerking back and forth motions these beautiful animals are subject to. You can hear their heavy breathing echoing and hooves shaking the earth below them throughout the arena. I found myself holding my breath and counting down the minutes to the end of the match, for the horse's safety. Over the course of most of the season, I was out there for about a half-dozen matches. There was one match that began the triggering of a red flag in me. During the fourth period of a match, a horse went down with a broken ankle.

Funny how this sport is usually played and paid for by the wealthy, but when it comes to an animal that is sweating their asses off for other's enjoyment, the decision point to save a horse with an injury, even a healing one, always comes down to money and rehab time vs. horse value, the perfectly chosen escape for humans to detach from justifying the responsibility they created, all in the hopes of avoiding any guilt, of course. But what these spoiled fools aren't realizing, is that it's already being logged into their own internal biology. Where it falls is their decision.

I waited and watched, and listened in. After examining the injury, they decided it was best to put the horse down. Really? The horse doesn't seem to have much of a say in this situation, not even a second opinion. The horse Vet is on-site for all the matches as an emergency, which is a good thing, but this sport of human enjoyment and competition looks a lot more like animal abuse when a death by injection happens as a result of their cute-uniformed ground-balling sport. Though the Vet does have the right to refuse if he feels he can help, it's also not a requirement. Ultimately, it's the owner's decision. Here's the worst part. If the horse goes into some form of shock and is laying down on the ground for a period of time, the circulation may be too impaired for drug transport to the brain and heart, with the veins being difficult to locate to administer, therefore a .22-caliber pistol takes its place to put the animal out of its physical suffering.

The women in attendance are just cringing with fingers crossed, hoping for the best, but knowing the truth all along when reality sets in. It's quite a heartbreaking ordeal to see a horse go down. If this happens, it'll be outside the arena, in back, as they attempt to see if the horse can slow-hop its way out with the team player dismounted, though almost impossible to remove the saddle during those moments unless they can still the horse and calm it down. It all depends on the severity of the break. But if you hear the shot, nothing matters anymore, especially the game. They try and tame their concern by saying words like unpleasant or unfortunate, and then resume the contest, trying to cover it all up as soon as possible.

Three weeks later, this happened again at a match where I was working the arena bars, but two horses went down this time, one in the third period, and one in the fourth. I guess this late-game indication of fatigue doesn't register to those who should be aware and concerned. Legs can get tangled and hit. One was saved and the other couldn't be helped. How I wish horses were smart enough to fake leg/ankle injuries, so they could be removed from the game to go back to their stalls after wipe-down, telling the players and this illogical sport to fuck off the whole trot back. I can only hope that what I witnessed was an extremely infrequent occurrence, but due to this sport being played all over the globe, I don't even want to think about the numbers, and I doubt if it's a stat the Polo world wants to keep track of either.

That was it for me as well. I couldn't bartend the polo matches anymore, not without the fear and grief. I grew up on a farm at an early age, so this unnecessary harm just wasn't sitting well with me. I kept on in other areas of the property for a while longer, but things changed and I eventually moved on to other bar gigs with more regular hours.

Today, my longtime bartending friend, Heidi Allyn, works over at the center taking care of all the horses and stables, which is perfect, as she lives literally across the street, has had a horse of her own forever, growing up with them in her family in New Mexico since she was a kid. She basically knows how to do everything there, as this environment is second nature to her. Heidi also helps out with many of the equestrian events that go on at the facility, including the annual William Shatner Hollywood Charity Horse Show.

22

THE TATTOO VAMPIRES

Annually in September, the Hollywood Palladium held the famous Inkslingers Ball Tattoo Convention and Tour over a 3-day weekend. It was the most prestigious tattoo expo in the world, with artists, exhibitors, contests, sponsors, merchandising, media partners, and even a Catwalk Xtreme Fashion Show. Open to the public with tickets purchased at the usual hubs, many celebrities would also show up and support the counterculture gathering.

Always a packed house, the doors to the event would open at 11:00am, and would roll on till about 11:00pm each night. Artists from all over the world and the Los Angeles area would set up their custom booth/exhibit spaces with different sizes, widths, and depths, creatively designed and colored out with special lighting and hanging logos and displays of work to attract and pause the endless passersby. An event of this size and nature, the day before is set aside for the complete move-in and set-up of the floor plan.

Traditional, old school, and tribal tattooing were practiced, and one artist with a big bed space towards the front of the stage on the floor used ancient tattoo techniques with old wooden tools. He was Polynesian, working in a way that reflected a great deal of history and experience with his craft.

There were three levels of booths in a natural circular pattern on the main floor, with the venue shaped as such, and the upstairs mezzanine section had more booths, as well as side tables and chairs to sit down and relax a bit. There must have been close to 100 or more in total, so walking around in this huge setting reminded me of the sound of locusts in the summertime in Arizona when I was a kid. There were millions of them. The electric toolage used for tattoos has an almost identical mid-range buzzing frequency.

The artists would have some client bookings already in place for the event, with open time slots allotted for walk-ins, and to kick back and visit with other artist friends that they may only see a couple times a year. People arrive, leave, and come back at all times of the day and night, so it's just a long ongoing party house. The only thing missing is a band, swimming pool, hot tub, and a retractable roof.

Cocktails are served. We're basically pouring a full bar from open to close right along with the festivities, with bars set up in about six different areas both in and around the main concourse, alongside the convenient flow of the walkways. There's plenty of food prepared out of the house kitchen, with variety kept to a comfortable selection of your basic cravings when you're out and about.

This glamorous theatre-like tattoo parlor is quite the visual spectacle to behold. Not only are tattoos being inked around the clock, it's also piercing central. I look all around my bar each day of the event, hour after hour, never knowing what body art I'm going to see in the middle of production next. There are a long stretch of hours in the middle where it turns into the ultimate creature feature. That period where the venue's house lights high above and wide should have a master dimmer switch adjusted to fit the changing moods with the altered states that shift energies into a higher gear.

Up on stage, there's a guy with a microphone in a quasi-emcee mode going over several of the day's activities, giving away free gifts, contests, raffles, as well as a panel of guest speakers during one of the days. The music is jamming throughout with just enough volume to sit over the top and drown out the sound of the constant equipment buzz to a degree that we don't go home with it humming between our ears. I do not want to sleep with tattoo dreams!

The slight bitch about these long-runner events for a nighthawk bartender is to get up and trek down to Hollywood before the sun has even reached the half-way point in the sky. My position and shift call time usually changed, no different from the other bartenders, sometimes closing one night and opening the next day. But Henry tried to work the dozen of us at times most suited for our preferred hours the best way he could, yet also considering the bottom line for optimum sales.

I had worked the event for only three years, but there were a few other bartenders in the bunch, namely Heidi, who was the longest-running bartender at the Palladium, had worked the event from its inception for close to ten years, so she knew a lot of people in the club and tattoo tribe. It was a fun, exciting weekend with a once-a-year event that was totally different from all the other shows, concerts, film industry wrap parties, themed/holiday events, music awards, cultural celebrations, and when the Pantages Theatre just up the street would rent it out for a party after a long theatre run. The thing about the Palladium is it was a good fit and central location for a wide variety of size-matched bookings.

It was pretty much rapid fire at the bars when it got really busy. Drinks, wine, and tap beer were flowing and going. One shift I'd be working with Heidi, the next day with Diane, and the final gig with someone else, usually putting the fastest, most efficient bartenders in the highest-volume areas. Henry was cool with putting experience, knowledge, and accuracy in the right spots, so I knew most of the time where I'd be placed for maximum service and ring.

I have one tattoo on my right shoulder, now 10 years old, a design symbolic of the breaking through of new ideas, a form of sacred geometry, with the center point of the bottom triangle piercing through the center point of the top triangle, showing a martini glass as a surprise result. The initial idea came from the logo and album cover of a British rock band in the 70's called Lone Star, who only had two recordings out, their self-titled debut, and their 2nd LP called "Firing On All Six". Down the street from me in Woodland Hills there's a parlor called Think Ink. My tattoo was done by a tall, long-haired, Harley-riding German rock n' roll guy named Uva, that I used to make drinks for at Palladino's Rock Club in Reseda. He was a quiet guy, but very cool. A tragic story. I hadn't seen him in a couple years after visiting a few times over some months shortly after he finished the tat. I decided to bike over to see if he was there at the shop while doing some other errands around the area, but his Harley wasn't in front like it normally was. So I go in thinking I'd just leave a simple message. I asked the owner when Uva was in next, and he looked surprised, then he realized. He told me that some months previous, Uva was killed in an accident while driving his wife's car through the Cahuenga Pass. I stood in silence for many moments. It's good I had my sunglasses on. I just didn't know what to say after "okay ummm, thank you", so I slowly walked out the front entrance.

On a Saturday in my second year of the event, the Cult Fetish Model and Porn Star, Summer Cummings, came up to the bar and flirted heavily with me while ordering a simple Cuba Libre, and handed me her business card. This hot, busty brunette with a killer bod and pretty face sent me reeling in my mind with naughty, but loving thoughts the rest of the evening. What a tease, knowing I couldn't leave the bar! She was a bad, but very playful girl, and to the point. Just my type! No beating around the . . . I still have that card today. However, here she is: SummerC.com – Brace yourself, you must be 18 and over to enter.

We used to sneak some shots and drinks here and there, you know, just to get in the groove with the crowd and loosen up ourselves. It always seemed to help the tip jar, so it was a win-win for everyone, though we had to hold watch for each other to make sure the chief wasn't lurking from a distance with suspicious eyes. We never knew day-to-day if he was going to be chill or wrapped too tight. It wasn't worth the risk, of course, but when you're breaking a sweat, ringing the registers up high and earning your bones, sometimes you just got to have one . . . or two, pending environmental variables.

During the last day of the event, towards the latter part of the evening, you start to see the slow shutting down, dismantle, and moving-out portion of the show, one-by-one, indicating the end of another successful weekend, looking forward to the next year to do it all over again, and again. And as bartenders, that's what we do too. We set-up an hour before opening, operate in full swing, break-down at the end of the night, settle the monies and either go out or go home.

After some 14 years of the convention, it doesn't seem to be around and running anymore. This event with its outrageous Hollywood atmosphere and huge enthusiastic crowds shut down its engines I believe around 2007, for no apparent reason offered. But its website was still up at: wwtattootour.com I kind of miss working the event, and though the Palladium is still open, it's now run by Live Nation, which from a standpoint of trying to get back to work there as an on-call bartender is now next to impossible to even find a way in, as they've barricaded the employment process through a website that just lists current job/position openings, with no way to communicate with HR unless they want to call you. The typical corporate wall of a closed house. Unnecessary, but standard operating procedure nonetheless.

Oh well, it was a good time while I was there. No, I'm not going to start singing "Memories"!

23

It Takes A Thief

If ever there was a slippery little criminal event planner deserving to be escorted North on a deep tour of the Mohave Desert in the middle of the night for a thorough talk and convincing to do the right thing from now on, it's this motherfucker.

I get a call in the last week of May 2006 from Tabi at Tender Bartenders for an emergency booking of a gig to bar manage a large event of 2000 guests in the first week of June for the Los Angeles Chapter of the American Institute of Architects. It was held just off to the North side of the 101 downtown, across from Union Station in the outdoor plaza and park of the old Los Angeles Historical District of Olvera Street, known as "the oldest street in Los Angeles", at 125 Pueblo de Los Angeles, between Arcadia and Cesar Chavez Ave. The original heart of downtown, and a block away from Chinatown.

I was aware of the general area, as I had taken the train many times to various destinations, to visit family and friends, and other times just to get away for a few days, to read and write on the rails, and to have lunch or dinner in the dining car over conversation with strangers of the same likeness. I would just take the 101 and get off on Alameda Ave, button hook over to the station, park the truck in the guarded structure in back, shoulder my backpack and disappear.

One of Tabi's bartenders, the beautiful, college-minded Regina, had been working the phones for her for a short period of time, and was assembling the 22 bartenders and 20 servers, but this size of a staffing job almost on last-minute notice can drive anyone in that position a bit crazy. There's nothing worse than waiting on call-backs, confirmations and details when it comes to this many. Such is the business here in L.A. that attracts a certain number of on-callers who are seeking Hollywood fame and fortune with every casting call they can line-up for themselves, but at times choosing to "perform" their real rent-paying gigs lacking the same drive.

I decided to trek down to the event site the evening before to view the staging and placement of the open space that was being white-fenced off to avoid the surrounding community thinking it was a free-for-all of food, drink and music. With strong security, there was only going to be one way in and one way out from a wide entrance gate, requiring an invitation pass to get in, and a convenient hub and drop-off point for valet to set-up and work the herd of cars and shuttles.

It was good that I made the drive down in advance, as the short streets and designated parking area was initially tricky to locate and maneuver with a couple of the normal passages blocked off. It didn't take me long to scan the grounds and figure out where the eight long stretch bars would more than likely go once I understood where the main gathering epicenter of activity would be, as the band and ceremonies that included the Mayor would be held in the large 5-step gazebo. Since the vendors and other event services wouldn't arrive for interior set-up until noon or so on game day, I hopped back in my truck and took off.

Josh was my co-bar manager on the day that helped out immeasurably, as we would end up doubling as barbacks over our early-in and late 10-hour haul. I got down there next day about an hour before our call time, around 2:30 pm, as with a party this size something is always bound to go wrong or off-course, and timing is everything, so extra cushion is necessary to help keep any unforeseen stresses and palpitations to a minimum. One of the reasons I don't do large gigs like this anymore if I can help it, praying that I'm happily booked somewhere else to avoid financial temptation. I've done so many of them that it just isn't worth all the trouble and no sweat equity.

The first thing I did after arriving on site was try to hunt down the ever-elusive event planner, Michael the I, whatever that title was suppose to mean. I went into a makeshift office in a nearby building and asked a lady sitting at a desk if she knew of him and his whereabouts, after I introduced myself. She said "Yes, he's about your height, and bald, but he broke his ankle yesterday so you'll more than likely notice the tender limp a bit easier". There were a couple dozen movers and shakers working in the plaza at the time, so I put my sniper eyes in gear until I eventually ran into him.

I had to get a credit card from him, as he failed to send a 50% deposit, or any deposit for that matter, of which he had time to do. Tabi gave me a head's up on what this guy might be like, and she was right. I introduced myself to him, and he did the same. He acted a bit flustered when it came to first-things-first, so as he pulled his credit card out of his wallet and handed it to me, he said with big town arrogance "Do you know who I am?" I said "No, I don't, and I've been in this business for a long time and I know a lot of people! Who are you?" Looking slightly uncomfortable when I didn't back down from his pretentious behavior, he zipped his card to me and continued by saying "I never pay deposits or anything in advance without knowing if anybody is going to show up, especially with a service I've never worked with before" I said "Tender Bartenders is the longest-running service of its kind in

Los Angeles. Requiring a deposit is standard practice of events this size, or almost any size for that matter. How do you not know this, after you've albeit reluctantly agreed to provide a deposit with Tabi in advance, as per her business policy?"

He said nothing and limped away in agony, asking me to return his card when I was finished.

This is the last thing I wanted to deal with as a beginning to the night. The stench of distrust penned the writing on the wall. I called Tabi and gave her the information from his worn plastic. She called back minutes later saying she wasn't able to verify over the phone that he had enough credit available for the deposit. Caught in a bind of bad timing for this to occur, it was either go with it or call everyone off just before the staff were about ready to leave their homes, or some already en route giving rush hour to the tight area of town. When you have 40 dressers ready for work, it became hard to turn back at that point, and who was going to go down the list and make all the calls?

We went with it, but I knew what was in store for me to have to deal with at closing time. I didn't let anyone know what happened except for Josh. The sole equal to confide in. We were in mutual agreement to just go ahead and nail the party with normal professionalism and service, and pull the crowbar out later if needed when no one else was around! So I quickly caught back up with Michael Broken Ankle, told him about his card issues, and kindly but forcefully demanded that he produce a check for the full amount at the end of the engagement, hoping he had the common sense to avoid any further injury to his person, though forgone conclusion of his ego told me otherwise.

There was a lot of work to do before guest arrival. But my job on this night was to be the master delegator. I took the bartenders, and Josh took the servers. Just beforehand, following the bars and back bars being set-up in their designated spots by the party rental company, the tubs, cans, and 4,000 pounds of bag ice soon

145

followed and divided to each of the eight stations dolly-delivered at fast efficiency, with a back-up in a dark corner area off the beaten path of the plaza. The liquor delivery came with $17,000 worth of product for a full bar presentation, nearly 180 cases of booze and mixers, also delegated to the bars equally in the same manner. Thank God we didn't get stuck with having to use real glassware. But just as stupid, the brilliant planner didn't fulfill his preferred responsibility of supplying the plastic glass bar stock, so he had to gopher a last-minute assistant to do so, of which he really didn't have, giving indication of his failed back-up contingency. And I wasn't about to make anyone from my crew schlep his duty for him. They had enough to do, and so did I. Smile!

The two girls in the office area acting like they were doing paper and phone work, were made to do the honors. Watching him wipe the beads of sweat from every face and head point of his slimy skull with his damp-falling handkerchief, I calmly walked off alone into the distance and dusk and lit up a smoke, though I needed another kind at this point! With only minutes to spare before show time, the operational lifeblood of any bar finally made it, and the glassware, once again, was delegated and divided accordingly. Imagining the frantic shelf raid at the stores by the girls, I wondered what credit card they paid with. Maybe they asked if they could write a check!

With this douche chosen and hired as the ring leader, you know damn well he received his huge deposit sum from the Architects Institute, and the entire remaining balance on the day of. He also took control of all purchases, instead of having the client write individual checks out. Therefore, the cheaper he could get away with doing things overall, the more in his pocket. He's one of those guys that will hardball-demand all the money he can get from the client up front, but hates to have the same demands put upon him from others. Most sociopaths don't! But a huge backlash came with the food that sealed his credentialed fate for the night, as he misfired on the numbers and covering his ass, something so simple if you're a good thief, but he was hamstrung with his own coin-tight habits, like a noose minimizing fluid to the brain, not mature and seasoned enough to handle the bigger picture, and getaway clean.

The appetizer alley was designed to work well, and though it did to a degree at the beginning, it looked like the cooking and pick-up station in the back wasn't at the size required to handle the capacity of guests expecting to have munchies flowing during the entire event. The passing trays were rectangular and a bit heavy. Michael created them from chunks of wheatgrass cut down to almost resemble little putting greens, yet a tad awkward for the servers to move in and out of the ever-growing crowd. They were also having a difficult time making it out and beyond the initial foodie runway to other parts of the plaza with a full tray, as many guests read the shoot like hungry wolves at the mission door. What Michael did essentially was show another rookie move, underestimating the amount and variety of food to be able to carry through to the end.

Josh was up on all of what was happening in this department and filled me in at different times during the evening. A couple of the executives from the Architect's Institute were furious with Michael and his shortcomings, demanding him to make it right or else. It's one of those cases where you have an event planner that wins them over in the office sales pitch, and fails with the on-site execution. Never embarrass the client! Hobbling around in pain and stress, he set his own instant karma in place that night. I knew at that moment I wasn't the only one wanting to create the sequel to Misery using "Michael the I" for Idiot as the linchpin character for Kathy Bates to reprise her role for bed-ridden terror.

The kitchen ran out of food a couple hours before it was supposed to, which is a long time in this business. Knowing things were headed in that direction, the catering manager had to make a run for the store with new funds to get a load of makeshift food to cover a little longer, mentioning to Josh and I beforehand that this was all the money Michael gave us to do the entire job with. This left many of the servers with very little to do for a period of time until things picked back up. But it looked bad, and the cooks and preparers didn't need any more stress put upon them when they're already slaving over hot stoves on a still, June night.

The bars ran well, with plenty of drinking as anticipated. I gave all the bartenders a detailed one-sheet set-up and breakdown of duties and procedures to follow from start to finish when they arrived, so I didn't need to verbalize too much. With two and three bartenders to each long station, they appreciated my simple and streamline technique of communication, and got behind the bars to kick ass and have a good time doing so, working with and for each other as any team should. I made sure they knew their roles and had their gear. However, there's always a few in the bunch that show up empty-handed, missing certain basic bar toolage they need to avoid asking another bartender if they can use their corkscrew. I filter them out, write their names down, and tell Tabi not to put them on another job until they have their shit together.

My job was to roam the bars pretty much all night long, and grab anything they needed from my remaining secret storage of back-up, and to schlep product and ice from one bar to another depending on which station seemed to be getting hit the most. Plenty of monitoring to do, yet still finding time to escape and observe the party from a distance whenever I could. This was usually the time when the thought would creep back into my mind of how I was going to handle the totaling of hours and monies owed at the silent ending of the night when I had to deal with Mr. Ineptitude!

The actual party went on from about 7:00 pm till around Midnight or over a little, per usual, with no fatalities or ambulance. A big party, a lot of people, things can happen. It's only when the place becomes deserted that you can see the clean-up disaster in full vision, like breaking down a carnival and moving on to the next town. One-off events are strange that way. It was weird that we had to leave so much leftover liquor just lying around in the open afterwards. Though gates closed and fencing surrounded, you know there would always be a way in if somebody wanted to find it. Once again, Michael had no plan or concern for the remaining hooch. His M.O. revealed itself to be that of get in and get out. I had no idea when or if the liquor outlet that provided the booze was going to come back for pick-up in the morning or later on that night after all of us had gone, or how long security would remain on-premise.

Putting everyone's time sheets together was not too tough. I had a master sheet for Josh and I to make things easier for the grand total. It came to $9,412.20. I walked into the office area where our queen of ceremonies was sitting at a desk with a laptop, leg up on a chair for the obvious reason, though he probably needed a hospital at that point. He had to have been on painkillers the 12 hours he was there, as he was spaced out and wired when I showed him the balance due, in full! He had a hard time looking me in the eyes during the close-out process. I knew Tabi and other vendors had his info as well, including his home address out near Pasadena, if necessary. A check was written in full and handed to me by the lady who had been hanging in there from the beginning. I then realized by reading the check that she was his conspiring sister.

I had to leave it at that for the night. The two of them packed up and left in this old beat-up 60's Chevy truck sitting just outside. Josh was out there waiting for me to finish. We both looked at each other thinking this was another bad sign, watching the event-planning version of Bonnie and Clyde drive off into the dark of night.

The next day I deposited the check into Tabi's business account at her bank in North Hollywood. She calls me a few days later to tell me that it bounced. Nobody would be surprised. Michael just wasn't operating in truth formula with anyone. I imagine he thought that he was good at what he was doing, but for me it was all too transparent to see. He failed at all the sign posts. Tabi then told me the final checks made out to the liquor service and food caterer were no good as well.

Later that week, the owner and his boys from the booze depot, and the food caterer, made special trips out to his home for collection. Michael was there. Feeling fear at the door, he paid up in cash for both the food and drink. We all knew he had the money, but was trying to get away without paying, thinking we would all go the legal route by filing claims with the court. The problem with this direction is it becomes a dead end. It's easy to get a money judgment, but the enforcement to collect in the State of California is really weak if almost non-existent. They should have marshals knocking down the doors and grabbing necks, but the State only does that for themselves, not for the hard-working citizens and small businesses. This is what Michael already knows, and what he counts on, the months it takes in court, becomes his time to disappear.

I remember talking to Michael's assistant, the French-sounding Wilfred, through his website email contact and by phone back then. He verified and confirmed his questionable business dealings, and felt really bad that he had any type of connection to it or him at all. Tabi took the court route and never collected, but has a lien on his home. I asked her why she didn't have the liquor guy do the duty for her while he was already out there, but she felt it best to follow her own due diligence. It's respectable and noble, but it doesn't get you paid in a timely manner. I told her I would take the paperwork and a couple Guido's with me and collect for her, thinking it only an equally fair action as he did for himself. She had to pay out everyone on the staff.

Shortly after that gig, he was already on the move to get an EP contract for a major event in New York and essentially attempt to do the same thing all over again. I found out what and who it was through his assistant, and Tabi tried to make the calls to the proper channels and give a head's up, but we never heard back on the outcome.

Michael's good at not leaving a trail behind him, even online. However, his sister is on Facebook, not hiding at all. Today, he may be doing more of the same, but in a slightly different capacity. As of a couple years ago, he was leading a group of individuals as Chief Executive of Fashion Los Angeles, trying to revive the city's exposure in this area, but it postponed until next year for lack of sponsorship pledges, hoping to raise $1.5 million. He also lost his partner and co-founder in the venture, who departed on November of the end. In an interview with the L.A. Times, Michael declined to say how much of the funding needed had been raised to date, but also mentioned this:

"When I took on his responsibilities as well as my own, running the office and trying to secure sponsorships, I started to think: 'You know, this is going to get sloppy,' and I'm really trying to create a community project that has years of repercussions and benefits. I'm not just in this for the money."

Believe me, the money is the only thing he's in this for. The last line of that quote said it all. But he's trying to reach a new number level now, so he can completely disappear this time for good, out of the country. Just last night, I spoke via email with a lady that was connected with the Fashion LA project. I thought the email addy would come back no good or something, but I actually received a response, and this is what she said, confirming my pinpoint suspicions:

"Hi Kyle, I'm no longer associated with Fashion Los Angeles in any way. Unfortunately it appears that myself and many others were taken on a con ride. Michael owes a lot of people a lot of money - and no one has had much luck contacting him. He's still at the same address as far as I know but both numbers have been shut off. Sorry to be the bearer of bad news."

Tabi then made contact with the L.A. Times reporter who covered the story. I made contact at the same time with another lady who did a piece on him and the organization in August of last year. The project has since completely caved in altogether and will not be moving forward, making the prior postponement meaningless now. His group's Fashion website is no longer online, and once again, has left no contact information. This more than likely means he won't be returning any of the sponsorship monies he/they did raise for the project during 2010, of which his business partner probably left to avoid being associated with him any further. I'm sure those company sponsors are searching for him right now, like so many others.

The Fashion Los Angeles Project is a great idea. They just had the wrong person at the helm.

New York, watch out! He liked to volley his activity coast-to-coast. So if you see his name around spewing kind words of business hype and trend, seeking funds of any nature, you may want to avoid pulling out your checkbooks.

He's been getting away with it for years now, and has yet to be brought to justice. Michael, your time is gonna come!

24

LEATHER AND LACED

Though I was floating around with some gigs at The Gardenia Room along with some part-time bar work at Shain's in Sherman Oaks, I was still in a strange state of transition after the end of a 3-year live-in relationship. I couldn't quite find a ground for myself. It took some time to get over and get past. It was early 1991. I get an unexpected call from my recent ex-girlfriend. It became sort of comfortable for us to chat on the phone now and then, keeping each other's spirits alive and warm, not falling into too long of an unnecessary funk over not being together.

As Sally was bartending at the famous Bar One on the tail end of Sunset, she hooked me up through a connection with the potential of a new, full-time gig at a boot-scootin' club on Ocean Park Boulevard in Santa Monica called Denim & Diamonds. I hadn't heard of it at the time, so I was game to check it out and happy for the link to something new. I think she may have felt that she owed me one, after I had the contact to the Bar One gig for her a couple years previous, through a friend of mine named Roger, who was bartending there while I was full-time at a bar gig elsewhere. Sally started out there as a cocktail waitress, but moved behind the wood a year later. It didn't really matter, she was beautiful and smart as she made good bank in either position, but she preferred the change when it became available. This was back during the early Roxbury days, and other clubs.

I went into the club on an early evening in mid-week. With a resume and app filled, I ended up speaking to a manager on duty named Glenn. We sat at a cocktail table for a few minutes as he looked everything over, and soon after I was put on the schedule for the usual trial run. That was fair. As long as I get a chance to prove myself, I'm good to go. At that time I had several years of experience, but the problem always was for me is that I looked like I was under 21. This baby face of mine was a mixed blessing. It always took more convincing in interviews for managers to believe that I was telling the truth of my early level of bar experience. It was always a nice compliment to hear when working "Are you sure you're even old enough to be behind the bar?", but it's also been the reason today that I'm more of just a grown-up boy than a full-time adult. However, the baby face is no longer a curse!

It was at a time during Denim & Diamonds' early going where it was starting to quickly grow in volume and gaining more and more popularity. Before it was D & D, it was a club of a different theme called Bentley's, but owned by the same nightclub group and in the same building that I believe used to be a bank at one time. The occupancy had to have been a good 300+. It wasn't small, so there was a need for anywhere from 8-10 bartenders on staff in various shift-per-week capacities to cover the rush of business, with a couple days off a week so we wouldn't burn.

We were dressed in our jeans, denim shirt, and cowboy hats. Since the club-goers were suited up in the same gear, it was impossible to feel out of place, and made it easier to fall in line from the more formal dress codes I was used to elsewhere. It was a good shell break, just what I needed at the time, something loosely tight. But the hats could be a bit awkward at times through regular adjustments and perspiration, and avoiding it banging up against the glassware hanging above the ice well where we stood and pounded out drinks like a high-paced machine.

Soon I went for a black cap that was lighter and not as tall in the hole that gave off more the style of a riverboat gambler, though slightly smaller, almost Chaplin-esque, to fit my look. I tried the standard Hank Williams/Lyle Lovett Stetson headboats, but it just didn't measure well unless I grew my long hair back again. Thankfully, my dark party hat passed as acceptable, but barely!

Speaking of Stetson, the famed hat house supposedly made its International debut into the spirits realm recently, and will be rolling out their Stetson Bourbon onto the U.S. market later this year, so watch out for it, as it could become a popular brand, and a nice holiday surprise gift of the spirit for any appreciative hat collector friend out there.

We had three bars – A, B, and C, spread out at perfect distance from each other. Fish and Terry were at C Bar, closest to the club's entrance. The four of us – Jimmy, Jeff, the beautiful Dawn (who was one of Hee Haw's Honeys during the last year of the show's run in 1992), and myself at the circular A Bar with four wells, parked in the center of the club. The hot, tall, curvaceous and busty Sheila held her own at the B Bar towards the back, in order to space the floor. She had an identical twin sister that used to come in once in a while. I could see how easy it would have been for her just to replace herself for a night without a hitch if she needed to in a pinch. No one would ever know, or care. It would have been quite humorous, had we found out. Don and Laurie were two other bartenders that were on the schedule who would mix in with us so we'd all have a couple days off a week.

I can see many of our cocktail waitresses in my mind, but can only remember a few names – Marilyn, Seldon and little Jo, our designated Jersey girl. Our funny bar backs, Jimmy and Chet, kept the ice, beer, and glassware rotating in a timely turnaround. The managers – Greg, Joe, Debbie, Glenn, and Mike provided all the duties and direction from on high. D & D, as it was known in short, became a popular chain of clubs, and though it made it all the way to New York City, the Ocean Park property was the flagship club which all that followed tried to duplicate.

We Rocked!

What we became was a club of legend. It's rare to get any bar venue to the point where it's busy 6-7 days a week, but we did it. You get the right package of personalities on the floor and in management, as well as club-goers, and it can set the stage for a long run if everyone sticks together. Not an easy thing to accomplish, or keep once you have it. Everybody has to take care and have each other's back. I was happy for the work. It got my engine pumped up again to normal operating power, and helped me relax and slowly begin to detach from my ended relationship with Sally, helped us both actually. We're still friends today, after many years of not hearing from each other, realizing we'd been living only a few miles apart almost the whole time.

One main ingredient that herded the volume of business in to a degree was the build-by-participation popularity of the country dance lessons that happened nightly everyday of the week. Couples dancing, the two-step, and line dancing became all the rage, a National phenomenon. The word-of-mouth benefit to the club alone was big. We would get them in the early evening, and they would leave late at night. It became such a social hang for everyone, incredible for its time. The club's bar and wait staff, and managers, along with all the patrons, became family after awhile, and many still are today, to the point of having reunions almost 20 years later.

It was also the type of club, though country-western themed, that didn't ring of hipsters only. All ages were welcome and felt an equally comfortable sense of belong. You could even have your boots shined from the two-seater parked just to the left of the entrance door. Eventually, as the word got out even further, the club hit its prime-time stride with major magazine and television coverage, coming in to do stories, high-end video cameras (state-of-the-art for the day, anyway!) roaming the club and in our faces and wells at the various bars while we were slingin' drinks and flippin' beers, cold Coors Light running like water, with MGD a length behind at a close second.

Celebrities soon caught wind, and we had a constant stream of you-know-who's walking through the double-doors in their best ranch wear, checking out the scene, getting in on the action when the mood felt right, or just to hang out, play pool and listen to the music. I remember when Marty McSorley and a friend came in from The Forum down the street in Inglewood, where the Kings and Lakers played, just after he got kicked out of the hockey game for punishing an opposing player. They walked over to me, my bar well facing the dance stage that night, gave me his credit card and proceeded to order beers and shots. I remember the night Pamela Anderson came in with a girlfriend. Plain-janed with no makeup to speak of, she walked over to me at the bar area facing the back of the club and ordered a Mai Tai, while her girlfriend stayed on the other side ordering a drink from one of the other bartenders. She still looked really cute *not* all dolled-up.

I remember working in the bar station facing Sheila at B Bar. A man playing pool comes up to me and orders a Coors Light. I immediately notice this huge nugget of a ring on his finger. I looked at it closer as I was making the transaction. It looked familiar to a ring that Lakers announcer Chick Hearn plopped in the palm of my hand just a couple years previous, when him and his wife came into Stanley's Bar & Grill on Ventura Blvd. in Sherman Oaks. They sat at the bar and had wine and a couple quick appetizers. It was a Lakers Championship ring. I inquired with this well-fit black man sporting a cowboy hat. We introduced ourselves. It was tight end Marv Fleming, who not only won Super Bowl rings with Vince Lombardi's Green Bay Packers and Don

Shula's Miami Dolphins, but was the first player in NFL history to play in five Super Bowls. That night, he wore the Dolphins ring in. I looked at it in amazement, then like Chick did before, he took it off and dropped it in the palm of my hand. If you've never had this experience before, the weight of these rings are like little barbells. The heaviest ring I've ever felt. Steadily, I handed it back to him with an appreciative grin of thanks on my face. He started laughing, gave me a nod of the hat, and went back to his game. Marv was 50 years of age then. He's 69 today.

Those short moments in time, provide the greatest memories. These are just a few of my many encounters at the club. All of us D&Ders at the time could fill pages with so many more of these same types of meet-and-greets. Everybody at the club was friendly and laid back for the most part, but occasionally there would be your garden variety machismo scuffle. It happens.

After the two dance lessons were over, the DJ's would start to crank up their music sets designed for fitting the variety of dance numbers for optimum floor fusion so the real hoofers could get their kickin', steppin' and slappin' on through the night. The choreography of the line dancing was quite an art to watch, with the regulars showing the newbies how it's done, and Gordie, Scott, and Chris shifting the rotation in the DJ booth. Chris, with his great voice over the microphone calling out the next song and dance, was initially one of our barbacks until he got his turn for more fill-in time spinning. Gordie slowly faded out of the mix, but would come back occasionally for a guest DJ spot here and there. Gordie also made Western Bolo ties on the side. I think I still have the one he made for me, must be deep in a drawer somewhere now.

Tracy Byrd was young and new on the country music scene at that time. He came in the club one night and performed a quick 3-song set on the dance stage around the time or just before he signed with MCA Nashville in 1993. Many other country stars of the day rolled into the club to hang out and enjoy the newest L.A. scene when in town. Even Hollywood night clubbers would come in and check it out. I could go on, but I'd rather all the D&D Alumna and Alumnus out there tell their own stories. You know who you are!

I actually liked country music, but preferred more the older songs than the manufactured pop-style that Nashville turned into, though much to the country music industry's benefit. I remember asking Chris to play "Misery and Gin" for me on occasion, as I really loved Merle Haggard's voice, but he had to put it on early as it was a a slower track. There was also a lot of George Strait, Garth and Dwight Yoakam played too. Mind you, this was also at the time where the music CD format had only been on the market since 88', so if my memory serves me, vinyl albums were still being used to a large degree, with CD's eventually moving into the circulation behind the DJ booth as more country titles grew onto the market as available.

With the consistent business volume of the club night-in and night-out, by the end of each and every shift, us bar slingers were quite the wired or tired bunch until we could calm down at some point later, just part of being a bartender in a big city. All of us would gather in a booth towards the back after bank checkout, and shared the count of our pooled tips, divided by the hours we'd work, as we all had staggered shift arrival times, totaled and cut the fair split, and high-tailed it out of there. Many times this final closing procedure would end at 3:30am. One night I could be working 7 hours, and the next night could be the long 10-hour haul from 4:00pm to 2:00am. It was the nature of the beast that we all accepted as is with no complaints.

The club was located within a large business office complex off the boulevard, full of buildings and open parking throughout. But way in back against a long chain-link fence was the Santa Monica Airport. A few of us (I won't say who) would go over there for awhile before the road home, to unwind, talk about the humorous happenings of the night, crack some jokes, talk shit, play loud rock music from my truck, and get high while watching the planes and jets land and take off into the dark blue midnight sky. It was amazing to see this strange amount of late-night, early-morning aviation liveliness going on over there, unexpected from a place that looked asleep! Of course, red-eyed and laughing our asses off like a comedy trio reacting to each other's cue, our first thought was that the airport's night use was for none other than illegal activities. I guess we felt right at home. We had our pipes and mini water bongs in use, and no one knew we were back there, except the pilots, as we had a six-story building hiding us.

My cocktail knowledge was about the best the club had, but it's not like we needed much anyway. This was way before today's "Mixologist" term came into play, not to mention the new cocktailian craft bars that have sprouted up in L.A. over the last five years or so, close to 25 of them now, including The Edison, Varnish, La Descarga, and The Tar Pit to name a few. The 80's and 90's for the most part were about the creation of fun party drinks, nothing terribly serious as it is now with the current herb craft uses of lavender, cucumber, mint, cardamom, lemongrass, an amazing new flavor variety of bitters, molecular mixology, and now, barrel-aged cocktails. It's become the new dawn of the artisanal bar. Too bad I didn't know then what I know now, or I would have introduced good, fun drinks more theme-related to the club, like the Horse's Neck, Moscow Mule, Border Crossing, Cactus Juice, Denim Lemonade, Cowboy Martini, Jolly Rancher Tea, Tumbleweed Morning Cream, Wagon Wheel Cocktail (to go with the Wagon Wheel Waltz, of course), and Solar Cowboy. A cocktail creator and designer since the late 80's, I made a few of my signature drinks at the club, but none more popular for taste and entertainment than my 5-layered super-shooter for four called "Blade Runner".

When Huntington Beach opened, some of the Santa Monica staff were selected to pull a training shift behind the bars there until the newbies got up to speed with pouring, procedure and things. Trekking down the coast, I arrived just in time to grab the only room they had left, on the D&D tab. I walked in, and it was this studio-sort of room close to the top of the hotel, conveniently right next door to the club. It didn't have a bed, so the long couch was going to end up being my night dreamer. The space was so cool and unusual, though, I couldn't get over it, with this low ceiling, it was like hanging out in a scene from "Being John Malkovich". If the front desk would've called and said "Mr. Branche, we have a more proper room available for you now", I would have said "No, thanks, this is just fine!" And weird!! I stayed overnight and left the next day to get home and refresh for the regular shift back at the club in Santa Monica that night.

The night of the drive-by-shooting was completely unexpected, especially in the area the club was in. The bullet, from what I gathered, or can't remember at all anymore, had hit the thick plastic glass in the corner of the club off of Ocean Park Boulevard on the North side of the property, where the actual Bentley car was once showcased. But it was loud in the club, and only the people in close proximity to that area had heard it. It was an after-effect for the rest of the club-goers in that night and time. No one got hurt, thank god, as I believe the bullet never made it through. The boulevard was an easy getaway for the shooters, with the parking lot on the other side being a bit of a navigational ground maze with vehicles in and around the main entrance. They wouldn't have made it out alive trying something like that there, and probably didn't know where it was anyway. Out over the grass near the main drag, the delayed reaction to it made it all but impossible for vehicle identification, even if the doormen out at the front entrance may have heard it as a loud echo above the background music on the inside. The squad cars came and did a full report. That's about all I know.

This whole incident, though, may have been a very late aftershock of the 1992 Los Angeles Riots, where the epicenter wasn't far away from us. I remember being scheduled to work on the night of, wondering if I should even go in. I called, but management didn't change anything. Against my better judgment, I drove over, up the 405 and West on the 10 Freeway, roads almost empty with a great deal of fear in the smoky red/brown air at dusk. I get there and stayed for awhile, but it was totally dead. No one was going out anywhere for anything in L.A., wasn't worth the risk. It was a very, scary situation here in town, like a doomsday thriller.

The club's heyday was in and around the early stages of California slowly putting the smoking ban in place that happened just a few years later. D&D had its share of smokers and drinkers, nothing new at the time. For any bar, fairly high ceilings in a club helped to a degree, but "second hand smoke" was just entering the discussion as the new catch phrase, primarily used by non-smokers. Some patrons did their pow-wow in a corner, some in the smack middle of the crowd traffic and movement, some sitting in a booth, and others outside the front entrance. We were covered! The ban itself had to do with the health concerns of workers. Bartenders and waitresses and the like were naturally moving more, exerting energies over great lengths of time, breathing more reps through the night. But with our club, there were a lot of dancers sweating it up on the floor with lungs pumping just as heavy.

However, this party house was also the chewing tobacco capital of the L.A. Club Circuit, "Dippin" they called it, with the city cowboys using their empty beer bottles as spittoons. Nice! But I guess it's better than having real ones in each corner of the club. Owners had a big issue with the ban, as expected, from a standpoint of business volume, or potential loss thereof. Funny how even human health becomes secondary to the dollar. In the simplest of realities, it was an easy fix. Just have smokers go outside and have a smoke, WTF! But we have to make it more complicated. In the end, and in hindsight now, it was all for the better. Now, smokers are happy to go outside to the patio, sidewalk, or whatever. A more respectable gain in public places.

Years ago, when I was bartending on-call one night at a Hollywood Palladium event, out of nowhere I run into Dev, a regular patron of D&D who I hadn't seen in forever. It was great to see her after so many moons gone by. Since then, we've kept in touch, and has led to the eventual networking of so many others from the past. I moved on from D&D in mid-late 93', a brief but sweet stay for me, but like all of my bar stories and encounters, you always want to remember the good times.

Of course, my fondest memory will always be of my girlfriend, Cee Cee, who was the primary dance instructor there for quite a stretch over that period of time. We hit it off really well and enjoyed each other's company a great deal. She was so strikingly beautiful, and smart, like PHD-smart! The energy between us at the time, it just happened so naturally, even though I may have felt like a guy basically from the other side of the tracks. She always dressed so fabulous and cool, and that body of hers! Cee Cee was one of the original OMG's of the day. I will always cherish my time with her back then, and we're still friends and keep in touch today . . . Gotta love that!

One never knows how long clubs/bars will survive with consistent popularity. You keep the train on the rails and it rolls as far as the steam and trend will take you. The great friendships gained between the staff and clubbers matched the strength and longevity of the environment's overall character. The reason so many are still in close touch today, two decades later. The onset of Facebook has certainly been a helpful hub and easy contact point in the last few years, and with ever-growing process, one never knows who's going to pop up out of nowhere and say "Howdy, Partner!"

Where are they now?

Richard (Fish) Fisher is bartending at Saddle Ranch Chop House up at Universal City, is a scriptwriter, and keeps in touch with Terry Lavelle.

Dawn McKinley was bartending at Fleming's Steak House in Woodland Hills last I heard. Hey Dawn, you better contact Hee

Haw. From an online source, they're looking to update current contact information on you, maybe in case of a reunion soon!

Jimmy Young, barback, now owns and runs a bar down in one of the beach areas.

Jeff Nimoy, second cousin (once removed) of Leonard Nimoy, is a voice actor, writer and director for various Fox Kids shows including the anime *Digimon*, and was nominated for three Emmy Awards in four years, winning once, for his comedic work as a writer and producer for NFL Films Presents on ESPN and FOX. He also co-wrote the animated feature *Pecola*, and directed the English adaptation of the Disney anime *Stitch*, as well as voicing one of the characters.

25

WHEN CORPORATE SAYS NO TO A GOLDMINE

"Like Little Works of Art"

Initially, I created my cocktail photography series so I could have my own drink pics in my then-new self-published work, some of them with a Western theme to fit the title and content of the book "Cocktails of the American West". Yet, I knew I was going to be continuing to shoot many phases in the series that would cover the basic categories of classic and specialty drinks in the hopes of using them in a variety of ways - images for use, postcards, calendars, U.S. postage stamps, jigsaw puzzle board games, and whatever else came to mind along the way.

One late night after a gig, I go into my local 24-hour grocery store (Ralphs) and head to the meat department to pick-up some ground sirloin to make my mother's goulash recipe at home the following afternoon. In the immediate area, there was a 36-card floor stanchion of dinner recipe cards, free to the shoppers, produced by a company out of Florida, Try-Foods International. I occasionally would take a look at several of them, in case there was something new that piqued my interest in the kitchen.

I'm roaming around the store picking up the other half-dozen ingredients while the night stockers in various aisles were singing in some comical harmony to a Journey song over the store's music station. Passing through the liquor aisle on the way to check-out, it dawns on me. I could do the same thing with the recipe cards but with cocktails. Paying for my goods, I was in a creative mindfire of what could be, going through the production in my head. I had known about these cards for awhile, as well as the latest cards they had in the produce section for salads and things.

The next day, I contacted my design/layout artist, Celine Luk (CelineLukDesigns.com), who worked at M&M Printing, just a bike ride from the house, on the boulevard. I had grabbed some of the sample food cards from Ralphs, showed them to her and said "Can we do this in house here with my drink shots?" Celine is so great at seeing the creative vision of others. She's always nailed it with my work and ideas!

This all started up around September of 2007. I had chosen 50 drink pics out of about 120 that I had at the time. My idea was two-fold. To have the variety of cards available individually for the possible future use in-store, and to create a retail product – a 50-card Volume I box set called Cocktail Art custom drink recipe cards. The first-ever P.O.S. tool and retail gift of its kind with the use of cocktails.

After speaking with Celine, Raz and Jason at the print shop, we were able to get everything done there, but the box set covers would have to be outsourced. It took some work and serious detail, but we finished the project in early December, just a few months later, and in time to have the box sets available as a cool new gift and perfect-fitting stocking stuffer for the holidays. It worked! Most of the units sold out from the initial order inventory, with a few saved back for other purposes I had in mind.

In January, of 2008, I made contact via email and phone message with Try-Foods in Florida to see if they'd be interested in working together in getting my drink cards out there, since they had already started the stream in with their food cards, and in searching on their website, I had noticed they didn't produce cocktail cards at all. I never heard back, even after a follow-up. The sense I got from them is that they were a very-closed house. They missed out.

In February, I contacted the Concord, CA headquarters of BevMo, sent the head buyer exec an email with product presentation and sample attachments. I followed up a couple weeks later to have her tell me "that since it isn't a product that we actually sell, it isn't something we would be interested in". In other words, the suits are shackled with narrow windows for expanded opportunities in generating more sales, even if she did see the potential when I spoke with her on the phone. I took the cards into one of the stores, but it's like talking to "obedient workers", even the manager-on-duty mentality was just "product-in, product-out".

In March, I contacted the main West coast headquarters of Southern Wine & Spirits over in Cerritos, CA, sending an email with sample attachments to an executive named Ira, the head of Wine & Spirits Education, about the idea of using the cards in the liquor and mixer aisles of grocery stores, etc.

I mean, after all, the whole purpose of this was to create a visual portal into the vast world of cocktails for store shoppers, where they could check out a recipe or two that they liked, on the spot, and purchase the necessary ingredients to make the drink at home, with those cards to take for free. It's simple, easy, and without the need of the confusing-to-some cocktail books out there. They can be just too much information for consumers, with hundreds or thousands of cocktails, where do you start? People just don't have the time for that these days with information moving faster than ever. I wanted to give them beauty and quality, quick and easy.

Ira didn't quite get it at first, it was so new to him, but after I explained in further detail, he loved the idea and asked me to send some to him in the mail. I sent all 50 cards with an empty card box, in case he needed to eventually pass them on through the chain of command. Having them shuffling in his hands to get that tactile sense going, that's where it hit home with him, seeing all of them at once, and its potential. Sometimes that's what it takes. He got back with me the following week to let me know he was sending them onto a guy named John in the Marketing and Graphics department.

A few weeks later I spoke to John on the phone about the possibilities. He thought it was a good idea as well, but through SW&S as the distributor, it would basically be giving all the sales reps in 30 states across the country another job to do, more in-store though, just a quick 10-minute in-and-out refill task, if they didn't create another position title for the upkeep and card fill-and-rotation of this new idea. How or if the many beverage brands would end up wanting to be involved was another question.

To have the brand names in the recipes on the back of the cards was an option, not at all a requirement in my point of view, unless they wanted to pay for it. But it's a sensitive issue, putting the brand names on cards, as you don't want to be turning off the customers. I would prefer the names off, and just allow the shoppers to buy the spirits they gravitate to, with no influence of any kind. And I wouldn't want to look like a sellout in the process, either. I'd be making plenty of money as is with the card's intellectual property user-fee agreements, therefore not interested in bending over for more cash, certainly not at the cost of ruining the shopper's interests and preferences. But it could also be out of my hands, if the user wanted the option at all times to use brand names in the recipes. Therefore, I would have to sign off on it simply in order to get the project going. However, we could have digitized the store's name in a small corner on the front of the card, with no issues.

John's department could certainly produce the custom cards in-house from the use of my master files, but it was a sizeable undertaking to consider, though the benefits of increased sales with the use of them in thousands of Kroger-owned chain grocery stores was tremendous, with the free P.O.S. product tool also being a complete tax write-off for them.

Everything about this idea had the word "Win" attached to it, all the way across the board, for the shoppers, for the stores, for the distributor, for the brands, and a huge, well-deserved and earned windfall for myself that I could simply keep going for years with an ever-expanding, seasonal and rotating selection of fabulous drinks from all eras of cocktail history. I really enjoy playing culinary photographer.

John said he would try and talk with the right people, but it would take some time. He still had to think it all the way through to actual process and usage on his end, who all would be involved, and who it would affect, before he brought it to the big table as a legitimate presentation package of value and benefit to the company.

I let some months go by to avoid being in anyone's face too much about getting it moving on the fast track. I prefer to have faith that adult business people will be diligent in their efforts to do the right thing, which is the wrong thing to do! In this crazy and questionable business world of ours, a 12-year old can be more reliable and trustworthy. Save the few, there's still just too much ego and arrogance in American business, in my opinion. But I'm all up for it improving, especially when it comes to allowances for people like me on the outside, yet who are very much on the inside when it comes to decades of experience and knowledge that I have to offer and give with all things bar and sales.

I finally make the follow-up call back to Southern to speak with John, and surprise! The receptionist tells me that SW&S shut down their Marketing and Graphics department, and John was no longer working for them. That move, no one in my position would ever expect to see coming. I wish I would have known earlier that it was dead in the water, but like I said, leave it to so-called professionals for proper closure with progressive, sales-generating materials in limbo. Just a call-back message, speedy text, or a quick 15-second email status notification would have been excellent, and very appreciated. Simple, right ?

The rest of the year went by, and in January of 2009 I worked a Super Bowl party for the head of a movie company, in Benedict Canyon. An early arriver was the famous actor/comedian, Jack Carter. He sits at the bar with Mark, and the three of us start chatting about the game. Jack asks me about the spirit, Lillet. I tell him a little bit about it, and that it comes in both blonde and rouge. He then, out of the blue, starts telling me about his old friend, Mel Dick, who is the Senior V.P. at SW&S in Miami, Florida.

I used that conversation, though I questioned doing so at first, as my beginning intro and cover letter to Mr. Dick, when I sent him a complete pitch package with product and samples, as one last ditch effort with the distributor. Low and behold, I actually received a cordial response via email, including a "Say hello to Jack for me", but no further interest could be done, more than likely due to the closures. However, having offices in many states, I don't know if they eliminated the department altogether or just consolidated in fewer places from lack of production, all depending on how much they did in-house vs. how much work they may have outsourced themselves.

I had read up on Mel's history with the company, as it's on the their website, to let him know how much I respected his close to 40 years with SW&S, where he basically started at the bottom, getting in with the help of others, and working his way up to the top. I wanted nothing more, if not less, than a similar chance to show what the cards could do in regards to increasing sales for Southern. The finished product was shining on the table. But that never happened. And I've never gone corporate. My idea has always been to work *with* them, not *for* them. Creative artists like myself have to be free. It's better that way for both sides.

With this scenario, it would be easy to see how the production and use of my cards as a P.O.S. tool could've possibly helped to keep the department open and busy again. John had my cards for several months before the shutdown, so it wasn't a case of too little, too late on my part. I did the best I could to help them recognize and see the vision and potential. Other than that, it was out of my control. From a cocktail/mixology standpoint, it was wide open with future progress. I'll bet none of Southern's "prized and hand-picked" house mixologists ever came up with an idea like this, and they have all the necessary tools and resources at their disposal. In my case, I took care of it all out of my own pocket, and on my own unpaid time. But they have their positions and roles within their extensive job description, that may or may not include a need or requirement for this type of creative effort, so no offense to them.

Who knows, maybe the four different places I presented the idea and actual P.O.S. product to just wanted to play it safe with what they had, but bringing mixology and the popularity of cocktails today more to the consumer/shopper forefront, and FREE in the aisle, would've been a perfect fit with current interests and trends. Without this attractive, educational tool that they could collect at home and put in their recipe card file, many shoppers will continue to just buy their bottle of whiskey or vodka, and go home.

My final move, I go direct . . .

In July, I make the decision to go in and speak with the Managing Director of the Ralphs grocery store that I've frequented for more than 15 years. His name was Steve. I introduced myself. In showing him the idea and product, he was already familiar with how the recipe cards operate and generate. What a breath of fresh air, someone open and understanding to an idea, but really in his eyes, merely an expanded one, but in the right direction!

I let him know that I wanted to do a test run of the cards in the liquor/mixer aisle, to see shopper interest and how well they moved. I mentioned that I had 500 cards, 50 different cards x 10 each. He looked at them, and liked them, as he could see how attractive they were. I told him that I would put up the cards at my expense, if he could supply another stanchion that I didn't have. He agreed, and a few days later I had a new set of cards printed and cut, ready to go.

I walked back in the store, met up with Steve, and we immediately headed over to the produce section. He didn't have an extra, empty stanchion to use, so we stripped the cards from the produce stanchion and moved it over to the liquor aisle. Easy peasy. I was in and out of there in not much longer than a half an hour. The set-up was simple. I chose 36/360 different cards to start out with to fill each of the slots, with 14/140 others as a back-up.

I told Steve that I would be doing weekly inventories, but this first week I wanted to check them every three days/twice a week. I had inventory sheets with every card listed so I could mark them individually, and had copies at the end of Weeks 2 and on, to give to Steve as full weekly reports, though he and I never really nailed down how long we wanted the test to go. It was open, but we needed to first see if they would warm up and take hold with the shoppers.

After the first two weeks, the cards did just that. 38 moved in Week 1, 38 more in Week 2, 19 moved in Week 3, than the big jump hit. 89 cards moved in Week 4, followed by 91 in Week 5. Week 6 went back down to 28 cards moved, but Week 7 jumped right back up to 55 cards moved. During these weeks I was running out of many cards and replacing them with the reserves, but the slots were quickly becoming empty. We also moved the stanchion every other week or so from one side of the aisle to the other, choosing three different positions to monitor floor activity for best placement and movement. In the final 10 days all the rest of the cards moved, well over 100, except for the 3 or 4 stragglers untouched after the stanchion had been taken in back, looking terrible on the floor that empty of card stock. Those last cards remaining I gave out to shoppers as I was walking out of the store.

The numbers were a bit all over, having to do with customer flow and shopping frequency. But all in all it was a big success, and maybe a surprise to Steve, but I wasn't at all shocked. I knew what they would do. I just needed the chance to prove it. The inventory analysis was pinpoint, and the numbers would have been greater if I could have continued perfect re-stocking of the best moving cards throughout. I covered all the main spirits within the 50 different cards, and they all went. I figured at this rate, with 500 cards moving in 8 weeks that with proper and expanded new drink card rotation and upkeep, approximately 4000 cards would move in a year, just in one store! How many extra bottles of liquor and mixers would be sold from this shopper interest to make great drinks at home? Each card would be pennies to produce with Ralph's in-house printing department.

Now, think of the entire Kroger-owned chain of grocery stores, thousands from coast to coast, of which Ralphs is just one of their many chain stores. The sales numbers would be incredible! What I also had in mind down the road was to have cocktail videos playing on TV monitors in the liquor/mixer aisle, and produce retail cocktail products to sell, like postcards, calendars, DVD's, fun inexpensive gifting merch for shoppers who happen to be cocktail lovers and enjoy the cocktail culture as another culinary door, along with food.

Steve goes to the weekly regional management meetings in Ventura and presents the P.O.S. tool with facts, figures, and even pictures of the stanchion. It falls on deaf ears, though more like the failed vision of executives, while they already had and allow food cards in their stores, with no brand usage on the back of the cards. Steve felt so bad about this, that he gave me the stanchion. I have it in the garage. Steve was my hero, though, because he was the person who *got it*, and cut to the chase to do it and give it a try, with no approval from above. Not that he needed any.

And so it goes. The recipe cards have kind of gone by the wayside, but not the idea of still wanting to get them out there. I'm always motivated, if someone else is. I can't do it all by myself. I did everything I could with my own time and resources to make all of these corporations more money, and they said no. This would have been my ticket to financial freedom, and a lot of fun future production of a great selling tool.

26

BONUS STORY

THE SLEEPING SPIRIT

JOURNEY TO COGNAC

Arrival

It's lightly raining. Off and on here and there. The perfect choice weather for me to enter Europe for the first time. Flying "over the pole" up through the top of the United States, over the Great Lakes, Hudson Bay and eventually above Greenland, I couldn't help thinking of one of my favorite movies, "Smilla's Sense of Snow". France gives one the feeling of an older world, like I stepped back in time. I looked forward to it. The mist and clouds followed us on the flight from Amsterdam to Bordeaux, landing safely after an hour or so in the air. It was mid-afternoon, and our shuttle to the town of Cognac was a nice drive through the country for another short ride.

I flew overnight from Los Angeles with three guys from Grape Radio; Jay Selman, Mark Ryan and Eric Anderson. Nicole Sizemore flew out of New York and met up with us at the Bordeaux train station, taking the train in from Paris. Working for the Cognac Bureau US /Carbonnier Communications, she set up the press trip for us, while associates from the BNIC (Bureau National Interprofessional Du Cognac) worked out our weeks' touring program and daily itinerary. I was asked to come along as the journalist/mixologist for the trip, while Grape was assembling video footage and interviews for what is now the James Beard Award-winning Cognac documentary "The Art of Blending".

Arriving in the village of Cognac, we were dropped off at the Hotel Heritage. It was so quiet, even if it was a Sunday. Odd that we left Los Angeles on Saturday early evening. Time changes I was used to, but entire day changes? A trip of this kind was long overdue. After some refreshing in our rooms, we met downstairs and walked to the centre of the village for a wonderful dinner at the restaurant Garden Ice. Here we had our first taste of the Summit Cocktail, made up of fresh ginger, lime, Cognac, lemonade, and a peel of cucumber. A great beginning of things to come!

After dinner, we took a walk around the village in the fresh night air and eventually found our way down to the Charente River, close to the bridge. We stayed for a while then headed back to the hotel as the mist was turning to rain. Half way back, looking up in the dark blue sky between the tops of some of the old buildings, we noticed for the first time just how close in proximity the largest of the Cognac brands are. Walking distance to each other like spirit brothers were the neon lights of Remy Martin, Hennessy, Courvoisier, and Martell. These four brands make up 80% of all Cognac sales worldwide. Even though there are close to 200 brands of Cognac, most of them are not exported. Next door, connected to the hotel was the Belle Epoque bar, but it was late and they were closed for the evening. No such luck !

River Town

Cognac is a "Royal City", with documented shipping to Holland dating back as far as 1200 years ago. There are twin towers that sit on the main street along the edge of the Charente. It was the original entrance into the village as it used to be a fortified city back in the day. Today, Cognac has a population of about 20,000 people. It sits directly North and East of the best vineyards of Bordeaux. And you won't see people running in the streets to their destinations for the most part. They take their time here.

The Charente River is a 224-mile long stretch where the Cognac barrel boats would take the cargo out to the shipping lanes of the Atlantic Ocean. Hennessy's longhouse barrel-aging cellars have been by the river since 1765, and is the only brand who's cellars still remain along the bank of the Charente today. It was easier in the 1700's for shipping purposes to the major seaports, but it is no longer allowed. Long before, salt was the first early commodity by the river, with under-ground cellars still existing up the streets today.

In the early 1800's, my great-great grandparents migrated from a town in France called Rosiere, to Northern New York in Jefferson County, an area upstate previously settled by countrymen who came over earlier and purchased a half-million acres in large tracts of land, up near where I was born in the historic Thousand Islands region of the state, close to Lake Ontario, derived from the Iroquois Indian word Kanadario, meaning "sparkling waters" or "beautiful lake". In reading through the family history on my father's side, many of the Bonapartists driven from France settled there. I also found out that some of my early descendents were soldiers in Napoleon's army. I guess you could say, for myself, France was a good beginning point.

Day 1

Monday morning's start of our itinerary began at Cognac Otard, established in 1795. Initially greeted by Karine Aiguillon, heading our tour was Brand Ambassador Nicolas Fagot of Chateau de Cognac. We arrived at the front gates in a van, though I was hoping to ride over on a horse with armor on. Walking in was like entering a castle of spirit, seeing one of the early pot stills from the past, the Governourship of Cognac Otard on the wall, and some tools of the old ways including a historic collection of antique barrel-branding irons.

We were then led into the original banquet/helmet room from the 13th Century. Francis the 1st was born here in September of 1494, and was a close friend of Leonardo Da Vinci, as many artists of the day were invited and made the trek to Cognac. They had some nice threads during the French Revolution ! We made our way up to the main hallway and Estate Room, where the special X-Y ceilings were designed for acoustic purposes. One could stand there in the middle of this long main room and just imagine the dining experience.

The barrel rooms were fascinating as we walked in. The air changed to dry and humid with a bit of a musty quality, the smell of old Cognac in the cellars. Natural for the contents in the room. Seeing the barrel stacks of cognac resting and aging together in their slumber was a beautiful thing. Each cask holds about 95 gallons, or 360 litres. The outside of the barrels are trimmed with sweet chestnut so the bugs stay away from the oak. And nearby, Nicolas showed us an old dungeon where enemies of the King would be sent, after captured, and left forever, never to be heard of again.

Down in the Paradis cellar where the oldest Cognacs in the world are stored, Otard's stock are placed in 34-liter glass demi-john containers. In this state of now being out of the cask (out of the woods), the aging of the Cognac stops. In the barrel, the wood breathes (air-in/liquid-out), the spirit lives through an evaporating process, with the loss being known as the "Angel's Share". Yet it is always transferred into the demi-johns at the perfect time. They look aged and dusty on the outside, but they're pristine on the inside. The 1795 Extra Old Cognac of Otard was chosen for the G-8 Summit when it was in France.

Heading back upstairs to some other levels, we walked into long rows of larger medium-sized oval-shaped vats that hold Grande Champagne Cognac, with round vats nearby containing Petite Champagne, In another huge room were the big Cognac blending vats. One could only imagine how important the frequency of consistent documentation is with the production and aging, and what's selected to bottle in any given year.

This was also the first of many tastings we'd be doing throughout the week. In the upstairs tasting room, Nicolas went over with us the varieties, ages and the individual qualities and characteristics of each cognac we'd be sampling. Some of the tasting notes including vanilla, coconut, floral, cocoa, framboise, and rancio were a true pleasure on the palate as we began to learn how to go about enjoying this time-honored spirit, educating us on the tasting properties. The word "Rancio" was explained as the aromas and/or tastes of spicy, honey, hearty, and cinnamon.

There is no distillation in the city. It is only allowed on the outskirts to avoid any major fires where the whole town could be in danger, since many of the Cognac brands are so close to each other, and would be doing their processes at the same time of year. As the harvest stage begins in the months of September and October, when the grapes reach their fullness and maturity, the brands have a legal deadline in the Cognac region to be completed by no later than March 30th. The growing regions total close to 80,000 hectares (approx. 200,000 acres), with thousands of wine growers. A unique aspect of the soil of Cognac is the special yeast that grows there, providing a complete and natural fermentation.

Being there in June during the early stage of field growth, I would love to go back again during harvest season.

Just minutes away was our next stop, Cognac Meukow, created in 1862. Pronounced "Moo-Kov", their logo, the panther, symbolizes beauty, elegance, power, supple and smooth. "Meow" to that ! Welcomed by Celine Coste Viard, we were then introduced to brand area manager, Damien Bertrand, who started us off on our tour. Arriving soon after was the president and owner himself, Mr. Philippe Coste, for a continued visit along with a discussion of some the history, and tasting interview.

Meukow's old Cognacs in their paradis are wall shelved and tiered, and kept clean on their exteriors. Their demi-johns are each wrapped in a canvas of sorts, covered to protect from the light. The over-sized corks at the top are replaced as needed. Many daily details to maintain. Meukow has 19 pot stills in its distillery, with their grapes harvested just before full ripeness. This exceptional brand happens to be more well known in the Far East markets, which is substantial in itself.

When the tour portion of the visit was finished, we were treated to a taste of an old Cognac from 1893. Quite incredible, aged, complex, and smooth. The expense is worth every drop. When using an alcohol made from grapes instead of a grain, you get more flavor because it's a natural fruit. Cognac is a living thing, and during its aging time in the cask it is in permanent contact with the air, allowing it to extract the substances by the Cognac from the wood, called "dry extracts", altering its physical appearance by giving it both its color and its final bouquet. This maturing process has 3 main phases: extraction, degradation (or hydrolysis), and oxidation.

From here, we jumped in a couple company cars and trekked over to restaurant La Courtine on the lake for a creative lunch and further conversation, with wine and Cognac, of course ! A history of sophistication in every glass ! When we got back to the Meukow estate, and before we departed on our next journey of the day, Philippe treated us to the making of a special pan-seared dessert with the use of Cognac as one of the recipe ingredients. Now that's the way to end a great visit and a wonderful tour ! Thanks so much to everyone at Meukow.

Our final stop on the itinerary for the day took us on a beautiful drive out in the country, to Cognac Frapin, which produces Grande Champagne Cognac only. Entering into the main property, it was easy to recognize how beautiful and manicured the surroundings were kept. Old buildings, but well taken care of. I'll take this over new and modern any day of the week !

One of the first areas we entered in was the tasting/blending room for the Master Blender, where we met up with Cellar Master, Olivier Paultes, who entered Frapin in 1987 and became the youngest cellar master in France, at 25 years old. Olivier's father, grandfather, and great grand-father were all cellar masters before him. Filled with natural light, this room helps with the color visualization of the blends, as well as measuring liquid/alcohol weight (density) of a spirit with a specific gauge tool called a hydrometer (alcoholometer). The lower the aging, the more blends you can put together. The higher/longer the aging, the less blends you can put together. With Cognac, everything is important; the level of acidity in the grapes, the wood used from two different forests, in the aging stages, etc. And all that is Cognac comes from Cognac. A complete in-region production, all the way down to the bottling (glass) and labeling (print). Even the corks are different. The oak casks/barrels that Frapin uses are all from the forest of Limousin.

After the video interview that Grape conducted with Olivier, we did a five-sample tasting of their VSOP, Cigar Blend – Premier Grand Cru, Chateau Fontpinot Single Estate XO, VIP XO, and Extra. Walking through the aging rooms, I was fascinated when looking at the large vats, as each are equipped with an exterior liquid measuring bar known as a "Site Glass", vertically on the front. Hopping into a couple cars with our luggage in the trunks, we then drove out to Frapin's vineyards, where we met up with the Director of the Domaine, Patrice Piveteau, who talked with us about the care and attention they pay to their grape fields, which when looking out across the land seem to go on forever. In the distance was a castle surrounded by the vineyards. Breath-taking to the eyes, surprisingly enough, ended up being our overnight quarters.

The stunning Chateau de Fontpinot.

Pulling into the entrance gates, we were greeted at the door by the President and CEO, Jean-Pierre Cointreau. The house assistants soon showed us our individual rooms upstairs, and we were to meet a half an hour later, about 7:00 pm, on the second floor living room, along with Olivier, Patrice, Max Cointreau, and other associates for a brief video presentation and tasting before going downstairs to the main dining room for what would turn out to be a spectacular 4-course culinary ensemble, wines red and white, and Cognac! We engaged in conversation about their history, our backgrounds and interests in knowing more, and future ideas for creative mixology using the spirit in a variety of cocktails for drink appetizers and specialty libations, potential food pairings, and after-dinner.

We concluded our day into night with dessert and some XO, with many thanks and compliments to the chef and everyone for their exquisite hospitality, and a place to stay. Just after everybody left that evening, we realized we were the only five people remaining in the Chateau. I walked outside to the front courtyard for some fresh air in the dark, quiet evening, before turning in. Thinking of the strong potential for otherworldly visitations, I started looking for a candelabra to walk up the spiral staircase with to my corner room on the top floor. They say ghosts seek beings with the path of least resistance. I must have ruined it for them. After a long and busy day, my weary energy had *no* resistance !

Day 2

Early next morning, the kitchen filled with the scent of breakfast croissants and tea. Like a scene from "The Illusionist", I was hoping my horse and carriage would be waiting for me outside ! Leaving with our XO Fontpinot gift bags from Frapin which awaited us that morning in an area underneath the staircase, it was sad to have to move on, as we would have loved to have the time to just walk into a sitting room and stare at the outside grounds for two hours, contemplating life. But the bottle itself had an embossed picture of the Chateau on front. Now that's a memory!

The morning van took us from the country back into the city. Over the bridge and on the other side of the river, we were welcomed into the House of Hennessy by their International Training and Promotion Manager, and our tour/education guide for the day, Jean-Michel Cochet. Hennessy has river boats on both sides, as their main office headquarters are back on the village-side of the river, where we initially started our week. Domed terra cotta tiles cover the rooftops of the longhouse barrel aging cellars located off the water, for gauging degree of temperature and humidity, assisting to some level in the cellars great aromas.

Cognac is the ultimate sleeping spirit. I mean, ask yourself for a moment. Where were you in 1913 ? All of us have the same answer. We weren't ! Yet, I'm standing here in front of barrels and demi-johns filled with Cognac that have been here the entire time. Amazing history, a bit staggering actually. But this is why so much relies on the handed-down education and know-ledge of the master blenders. There are generations of tasting blenders always in training for the future; two in their 60's, two in their 50's, two in their 40's, and two in their 30's. Their knowing of when to switch the eau-de-vie from newer barrels that give more color and flavor aging quicker, to the older barrels that take longer to color and age, all due to the breathing qualities and properties of the oak wood, which are water tight, but not air tight. Essential for just the right amount of resting, blending, and aging. The quiet time of marriage together.

Hennessy uses four ages of barrels – 1, 2, 5, and 10 years. On those barrels they still practice the writing art of calligraphy, with initials, names, and dates all written in chalk, reflecting the finesse and strength of ancient times. Part of a long tradition of perfection. Collectively, with all the Cognac brands, the annual evaporation losses from the aging process in the barrels equates to roughly 27 million bottles each year. Close to a wholesale loss (or non-gain) of about a half a billion dollars, if my tumbling is accurate. Though these are serious numbers, it still only results in 2-3 percent of the total Cognac production. In a 2007 report, total Cognac shipments were the equivalent of 174 million bottles, resulting in 5 bottles of Cognac being sold every second throughout the world, representing 1.5 billion euros in France's trade balance. More than 21,000 people work to produce and market Cognac, sold in more than 100 countries.

After a boat ride up the river, we headed back to the village-side and entered the main building of Hennessy headquarters. So much history! Jean-Michel took us up to the museum section for a look at both the past and the present, including a tools of mixology exposition dedicated to professional bartenders of the culinary art everywhere, old bar books, historic antique cocktail shakers, and the like. The perfect timing and resting place for my new and unique gift to Jean-Michel and the Hennessy Museum, my latest bar product release, the "Original Cocktail Art Custom Drink Recipe Cards" – Volume 1 Box Set of 50. If I wasn't before, I am now officially in the annals of bar and cocktail history, in Europe !

Enter the tasting room, with the Director of Research and Enology, Mr. Laurent Lozano. Complete with our own individual spittoons, we were ready to go with eyes and ears open. We began with a spread of 10 different gradations on each of our desktops. Starting with the young, colorless eau-de-vie, and ending with the darker, most-aged Cognacs. Eau-de-vie, said Laurent, "is the beginning, just distilled spirit, before aging begins. The child spirit that grows over time". This is where you can really notice the tasting and aroma variance, the subtle characteristics. But it starts at tasting glass #2, as the #1 eau-de-vie is the unaged "fire strength" spirit at about 140 proof / 70 % ABV. The distinct tasting notes I recognized with #4 really hit home with me (medicinal, floral, cocoa) as far as a stronger understanding or sensing of the true differences between floral, fruity, woody, and rancio (spicy).

With the nurturing of the grapes during the daylight hours (Solar Time), I couldn't help but to question what benefits the night hours (Lunar Time) may have on the grapes and vines, and the Earth. My guess is the same as when the eau-de-vie is aging in an oak cask for designated periods of time. It's sleeping in the dark. In the daytime is when the Sun's active energies are nourishing the fruit, alive in the fields. In the blue nighttime sky is when the cooling and resting energies take over, to prepare for the next day's growth of activity, all the way to harvest.

After our tasting class, it was time for some nourishment ourselves. In the van again we went, with lunch being offered by Hennessy at their fabulous guest house, the Chateau de Bagnolet. These are more like "guest mansions", a little different than the American version of a guest house. With sprawling grounds in the backyard all the way to the water nearby, it was complete with a bartender on the outdoor patio preparing Cognac cocktails for us before we went in to eat. Very refreshing start, before yet another superb 4-course meal. We should all live like this !

Right across from the front drive/entry way through a gated entrance, were the vast Hennessy grape vineyards. Many thanks to Jean-Michel and his exceptional service staff, for an incredible afternoon of food, drink, conversation, and education. And by the way, Laurent came in on crutches from injuring a knee during a soccer match. We appreciate and applaud his extra effort.

Between the Hammer and the Anvil

Off we went back out to the country for a 30-minute drive, which was a very pleasant respite in itself. Heading toward the next stop on our tour, we arrived for a 1½ hour visit with the manufacturer of Cognac's alembic pot stills, Alambic Pruhlo, and their Commercial Director, Philippe Tizon. Walking in and observing from a distance for the first couple minutes, we learned that the artisanal method of building them from scratch hasn't changed in close to 200 years. Though all stills are made from intense manual labor, there's something to say about that homemade feel in the end product.

Hammering into shapes and design sizes for the different parts involved is a precise and methodical process. Stills are made of copper, and all the copper used in production comes from Chile. The ability of making the copper, and therefore the still, a very pure piece, is obtained by electrolysis, treated to tighten its pores, increase its mechanical resistance, and make it smoother and easier to clean. The smoothening out of even the slightest inside bumps, again with a gentle but strong finesse with the hammer, is essential in the overall completion of each piece. Years of experience helps to feel where to gently hammer when you can't always see where you're hitting.

The bottom pot is 12mm thick, for a good quality of heating. The middle and top dome of the onion-shaped still is 3mm thick. All in all, this results in a better quality product and eau-de-vie. Put together by two rows of rivets very close, the holes are drilled about 1-1¼ inches apart. Then you have the condenser, the connector tube, and the serpentine copper cooling coils. They first finish the full assembly here at the main production plant, then do the liquid testing at both extreme temperatures, as water quality is very important to the spirits. From there, they disassemble, ship by truck to the distiller/client, then re-assembled on site. Each alembic pot still system costs approximately 100,000 euros. Thanks to Philippe and his impressive and patient working staff, for allowing us in to observe and learn during their regular, daily production load.

On our way back into town, we spirits travelers arrived at the next and final stop for the day, at the estate of Courvoisier Cognac. Welcomed by Trade and PR Manager, Jennifer Szers-Novicz, and Director of Operations, Patrice Pinet, we were given keys to check into our rooms and to meet back downstairs in 30 minutes for the start of the tour and tasting. Very nice accommodations, and again I had a corner room, with a beautiful overlook of the Charente River.

We started out with a walk-through of Courvoisier's museum section, where you see many old tools and artifacts used in the past. What I noticed at the far end of the room was a large glass-encased sample of an in-depth look at the chalky, rocky, limestone earth where the grapevines are nurtured for Cognac. Yet, the specific grape varieties of mostly Ugni Blanc and maybe a small amount of Colombard are what work best for the aging into Cognac, as they have good levels of acidity and are low in alcohol content. Sauvignon Blanc and chardonnay grapes don't work well for aging as a Cognac, as it loses some essence and quality, where as the Ugni grapes hold up better. To go slightly one step further, during the early crushing and de-stemming phase, some brands choose to keep some grape leaves in during the process, depending on blending preferences. Courvoisier is contracted with about a thousand independent vine growers in the region, growing grapes for their brand. Now that's what I call working with the community!

Especially interesting was the section they had on Napoleon himself, including a dresser, clothing, shoes, and a small bed used during the war. Being the creator of the "Napoleon" quality Cognac, a scaled down version of the bureau along with a bottle of a special Napoleon blend that fits inside, has been produced as an exclusive gift package. A superbly attractive specialty item. From the museum we walked down and around to the beautifully-lit barrel aging rooms, turned a corner and stepped into a special sitting room for a video presentation, with this unique oval-shaped viewing screen. A first time for everything !

After the viewing we followed Patrice upstairs to another part of the estate, the Courvoisier tasting room. Enjoying samples of six different house Cognacs, Patrice led us through and explained the tasting notes and qualities unique with each aging, from rancio, V.S., V.S.O.P., Exclusive, Napoleon, and XO Imperial. I remember certain flavor aromas on the nose that brought back distant memories from my childhood, something familiar from the past that I can't quite put a word on. It must have been an earthy quality that connected to the farm I was raised on as a child. Trees, woods, tall grass, the lake, the soil, the fields, the sky. For me, going to Cognac was in many ways, going back home to where it all began.

The great thing about all of these brand tastings is, we get to familiarize ourselves with the characteristic differences between them as well. Recognizing the master blenders as the architects of their brand's individual quality and distinction, painting a landscape of flavor and aroma for the palate, and to enjoy the history and passion with this "spirit of the soul", Cognac. Blend – Color – Aroma – Body – Taste – Finish . . . . .

Heading back, we made a stop into the sun-filled blending room for a few minutes, where the light was right for the guys from Grape Radio to conduct another of many important and necessary interview sessions for their documentary work in progress. Such a great team we were to tour together from our three different areas of work within the industry, as it allowed the five of us the opportunity to learn a little bit from each other's work. I noticed some bottles they had on a counter where the labels were upside down. Patrice informed us that the U.K. bars use 1.5L bottles in their massive liquor trees, upside-down of course. Made sense now!

Enter paradise. Jay Selman of Grape turned the magic key and we entered into Courvoisier's cellar of the old. In here, the past is alive and well ! Dark, musty, humid. Perfect resting place for these rarities. There are bottles here in their paradis, from 1783. The room is also filled with oak casks and demi-johns. If there's anyplace where cobwebs can be cool and groovy, it's here.

Our tour ended, and we headed to the downstairs bar and lounge area in a main lobby, where the house bartender mixed us up a couple different Cognac cocktails for the 7 o'clock hour. Getting back to our rooms to freshen up and a change of clothes, we headed down a floor in the elevator to our table of seven set in the main dining room. Four-course meals to this degree is new for me, much less every day on the trip, lunch and dinner. The meal was excellent, and very appreciated. Bravo to the chef, waiter, and bartender. We enjoyed each other's company and conversation over those two hours, sharing thoughts and observations, with interesting questions too. Later with Cognac in glass, we moved over to an adjacent room for relaxing a bit. A piano was in the distance, and the space was filled with beautiful furniture, interesting objects, and many other collectible luxuries, reminding one of walking into an antique store. A very charming room. There was another early morning coming around, so after a while I headed back up to the room to get in some serious snooze time, as my normal night hawk hours were turned around a bit.

Day 3

Heading out with our guide during the day, Beatrice Bernard, we snuck in an early morning visit on our itinerary to an independent vine grower in the Cognac region. Michel Guilloteau comes from a family of winemakers and growers who's soil is full of limestone, essential to produce Cognac. They have been in their village since 1744. Jay and Mark set up in one of the very clean rows in his fields of green and conducted a great interview session. Michel spoke very little English, so Beatrice stood close by for translation, and Eric and I shot some photography of the lush hectares from a distance. Though Michel loves tending to his fields, there are no relatives who wish to take it over when he retires. So he continues . . . . . Cheers to him!

Growing Areas (The Crus)

The Cognac production area was delimited by the decree of May 1st, 1909. Six Crus were then ratified by decree in 1938. These areas in the Delimited Region reference the following appellations and their individual soil characteristics:

GRANDE CHAMPAGNE

The most prestigious Cognac vintage, with a soil called the "Campus" (where many fossils are to be found). The quality, complexity, and longevity of the spirits that come from this region are unequaled anywhere in the world. Producing fine, light Cognacs with a predominantly floral bouquet, which can turn into fruity aromas as they grow and mature even after aging. These white wines require long aging in casks to achieve full maturity.

PETITE CHAMPAGNE

Very similar eau-de-vie to that of Grande Champagne, but without its finesse. A large semi-circle area who's "Santonian" soil (chalk of Saintes) is rich in limestone, with a floral and somewhat fruity scent, but a much shorter bouquet.

BORDERIES

These vineyards to the North of Cognac produce nutty-flavored spirits on a decalcification soil. Its soil contains clay and flint stones, that are the result of decomposing limestone. Though the smallest of the 6 Crus, their vines produce fine, round Cognacs, smooth and scented with the aroma of violets or irises, reaching an optimum quality after only a short aging period. Some houses use it as a base for their best Cognacs.

FIN BOIS (Fine Woods)

Surrounding the above 3 Crus, this large growing area lying in the lower countries is covered by clayey, chalky soils of red color and hard stones, producing smooth, fairly quick-aging Cognacs with a bouquet reminiscent of fresh-pressed grapes.

BONS BOIS (Good Woods)

Sandy soils are found in this Cru, whether it be on its coastal side, its valleys, or on the Southern part of the vineyard. The vines here are dispersed, mixed with other crops, and surrounded by forests of pine trees and chestnuts.

BOIS ORDINAIRES (Ordinary Woods)

Another sandy-soiled region of only 1,100 hectares of vines, lies along the coast or on the islands, producing a fast-aging eau-de-vie with a characteristic maritime flavor. Both Bons Bois and Bois Ordinaires regions are made up of clay soils that are less in limestone levels.

FINE CHAMPAGNE

This area is not a Cru, but a controlled appellation composed of a blend of Grande and Petite Champagne eau-de-vie, with at least 50% Grande Champagne.

NOTE – 1 hectare = 2.47 acres

Earth, Wind, and Fire – A visit to the Cooperage

Loaded back into the van, we motored on for another twenty minutes of country roads, and pulled into the parking area of Tonnellerie Doreau, the workshop and facility that assembles the oak casks, from forest to barrel.

The French oak trees come from the forests of Limousin and Troncais, which lay Northeast of the district, in the Cognac region. This is the type of porous, breathable quality of wood that provides so much of what is Cognac, quite low in the harsh tannins that can be a little too bitter to a young brandy. Troncais produces a soft, finely grained wood where the tannins are smooth, while Limousin produces a medium-grained wood, a bit harder and prized for the strength and balance it imparts.

Off in the distance on the property were the massive logs which gets everything started. Initially, it gets to the log splitter, a very loud and large machine tool. The cooper was a patient and kind operator of the power tool, showing us an example of how it worked with a real log split. He quickly made us comfortable as he was in good cheer singing something operatic just over the sound of the machine. It was a bit frightening at first, being ten feet away, but we got used to it.

These still-skinned pieces are cut to a certain spec, then carted off to another area of the facility where the table saw operator skins and further cuts them into exact size planks (or staves), then put in large tied bundles and taken back out into the open air for the "drying out of the shook", stacked to weather-age for 2-3 years, releasing any unwanted substances within the wood when cut fresh. For a moment following the stand-up slice performed by the splitter, Mark asked the cooper to go into Texas (or Paris) chainsaw mode and cut a chip and leave it hanging up between the two big logs. Very cool, and Mark caught it on video.

Watching a from-scratch barrel prep was pretty amazing. The cooper used 30 planks, lining up within the confines of a bottom ring (barrel strap) to hold them together. On the last plank, he had to slide it down between the rest of them with some gentle force, but the circular fit was perfect. I couldn't believe what I saw as they came together like that, right before your eyes, like a form of magic. From this phase, they get turned upside down and slowly rolled over a fire for a determined period of time, for what's known as the "barrel toasting". Toasting the inside of the barrel not only heats the staves for softening and bending purposes for the eventual barrel strap over the top, but toasts and therefore darkens the wood on the inside to the correct degree that helps in the aging and tasting complexities of Cognac. Slowly, these wood planks will warm together and bond for life.

From the fire phase, the barrel gets rolled over to the cooper in charge of measuring and centering the spot for the drilling and burning through of the bunghole. The fitting, insertion, and sanding of the barrel covers is followed by some hammering and laser-measuring of the barrel rings/straps, lining both of them up to spec. The barrel goes through a balancing test, as well as some possible light hammering on the inside to smoothen out any small, rough spots. The liquid testing is done for the obvious reasons of creating a water-tight seal with no leakage.

Splitting, cutting, sawing, measuring, fitting, heating, hammering, strapping, sanding, drilling, and testing. It's all part of the process. Quality control of each piece and of every phase of production, at a cost of about $900 a barrel. Upon our departure, we thanked everyone for their time and allowing us to come in for a visit and education of this time-honored craft, as they were in the middle of another busy day of barrel-making.

We then headed back into town and over to our next stop, the BNIC, Bureau National Interprofessional du Cognac. who sponsored our trip. Introduced to Jerome Durand, former Director of Marketing, we made a quick drive over and around the corner for lunch, cocktails and discussion at the Bistro des Quais, where we were again treated with the Summit Cocktail and appetizers at the start of our dining experience. The cocktail was created by bartenders invited to the International Cognac Summit held in January of 2008. Arriving back to his office in the BNIC building, the guys from Grape conducted a video interview and radio segment with Mr. Durand as the end portion of our visit with them.

Off we went on our first walking tour in the village, starting with a visit to MACO, the Museum des Arts du Cognac. We didn't do any video or photography in the museum, nevertheless had an enjoyable time looking at all the past-to-present history of this legendary spirit, the village, and its people. After that, we set out on a guided visit to the Old City of Cognac, led by Michel Goubard, Cognac's Director of the Office of Tourism. It was a sunny and beautiful afternoon out on the walk through the narrow, winding streets of its old town, of which the stonework of its old houses often coated with a black velvet, the work of a microscopic fungus that feeds on alcohol vapors. Each day while we were there, the weather became better and better. Working off some calories and breaking a little sweat felt good, then we strolled over to a nearby park for some rest and relaxation for a spell. Michel showed us a stage and amphitheatre-styled lawn in the distance where they have numerous Spring/Summer events, including the Blues Passions Festival in August and the "Coup de Chauffe" Street Theatre Festival in September. Too bad we were leaving before Sunday !

All of our luggage was in the van and ready to go when we got back to the BNIC headquarters. Before we headed back to Bordeaux later that evening, we were lucky to have just enough time left to trek through the countryside and over to the home and vineyards of Paul Giraud, for a visit with the man and his Cognac, who's family has been growing grapes since 1665. He created his own brand in 1976.

With only an hour or more, Paul took us out to his vineyards to see his grape vines. His fields, a little over 86 acres in total, surround two sides of his home, and are situated in the heart of the Grande Champagne in the village of Bouteville. Paul was great to talk with, and had a fun, passionate and humorous personality. He talked of the vines, leaves, and fruit, describing them as beautiful girls who need water, nurturing, attention, and energy from the sun to grow proper and strong. A vine who's leaves are of a rich, green color is getting its nutrients, but the vine next to it or a few feet over, its leaves could be of a lesser shade of green and not quite receiving all that it needs. Even so, when the vineyards suffer, they still produce a good quality. With the soil being the perfect type for growing grapes, the vines are strong and tough, and can handle some weather. We noticed snails on some of the vines, as Paul mentioned that the area was a sea at one time.

Each vine produces many a grape, and that's a good thing, as one batch of full-grown grapes can yield one liter of eau-de-vie, but it takes 10 liters of that to produce one liter of Cognac. The terroir is rugged, and you only have to re-plant about every 40 years, or twice in a lifetime. Grape shot their last interview with Paul while we were out in the fields. Heading back to his house and sitting down together in one of the living rooms on the main floor, we did a tasting of his special line. The sun was shining through part of the window, giving us perfect light to view the color-aging of the various selections, as well as the taste! Paul said "Cognac is a combination (or collection) of memories in a bottle. From the past, the present, and into the future". I couldn't agree more!

It was so nice to have the time to stop by, worth every minute! Thanks to Paul for taking time out of his busy day, and patient thanks to our van shuttle driver who then took us to the airport hotel in Bordeaux for the night. We arrived just in time to have one last meal together, as my leg of the tour was completed. Nicki and the guys from Grape toured on to some wineries in Bordeaux for the next couple of days, then Nicki took the train back to Paris to visit some friends, before heading home to New York. I flew off the following morning to Amsterdam (damn, not enough layover time to take the train into the city for a quick cafe excursion!), and then onto Los Angeles. What a great tour this was. I think I slept about 20 hours in the whole time there!

Websites

NIC – Bureau National Interprofessional du Cognac –
   cognac.fr
Carbonnier Communications – New York –
   carbonniercommunications.com
Alambic Pot Stills – Groupe Nov-Tech – **groupe-novtech.com**
French Oak Barrels – Tonnellerie Doreau – **tonneau.com**
Grape Radio – California – **graperadio.com**
Office de Tourisme de Cognac – **tourism-cognac.com**
MACO – Museum des Arts du Cognac – **musees-cognac.fr**
Cognac Otard – **otard.com**
Cognac Meukow – **meukowcognac.com**
Cognac Frapin – **cognac-frapin.com**
Cognac Hennessy – **hennessy.com**
Cognac Courvoisier – **courvoisier.com**
Cognac Paul Giraud – **cognac-paulgiraud.com**

Purchasing Cognac

V.S. – Very Special – At least 2 years, usually 5 Years Aging
V.S.O.P. – Very Special Old Pale – At least 4 years, usually 7-10
   Years aging
X.O. – Extra Old or Napoleon – At least 6 years, usually 15-25
   Years aging
Grande Reserve – Up to 50 Years Aging

NOTE –Cognac Master Blenders will usually use eau-de-vie that are much older aging than the minimum requirements for their bottle blends. In 2016, the X.O. category will have a new designation to be at least 10 years aging.

ABOUT THE AUTHOR

Kyle Branche is a 30-year veteran professional and private bartender in Los Angeles. Originally from the historic village of Sackets Harbor, off the edge of Lake Ontario in the Southern part of upstate New York in the Thousand Islands region near Cape Vincent where he was raised on his Grandparents' dairy farm up until the age of seven. From there he moved out West to Arizona, though went back in the Summertime of his early teens to vacation and help with the farm chores of driving tractor, cutting fields, baling hay, feeding cows, and riding the farms' Honda 70 motorbike anywhere and everywhere.

While in Phoenix as a rack jobber in the music business, where he received sales display awards from Columbia Recording Artists, Journey and Willie Nelson, and then as a manager of a computer warehouse, he also moonlighted on the weekends as a barback at an establishment nearby where he lived. He then got hired at a brand new Embassy Suites Hotel, eventually transferring to Los Angeles and the bigger bar scene in 1985.

His wide variety of bartending experiences in the City of Angels is second to none, having worked in many bars, nightclubs, private clubs, restaurants, hotels, concert venues, and is currently more off the grid today working a busy, yet more flexible schedule as a private on-call bartender with a variety of services, caterers, event planners, brand-sponsored events and private clientele working the party circuit throughout the spread out metropolis. while still holding position in the bar at The Gardenia Room in Hollywood for 22 years. His Blog of stories and encounters is culled from many moons behind the bar, now in his fourth decade.

Kyle was a contributing writer and columnist in the leading beverage magazines from 2002-2012, with 75 published pieces, including the monthly cocktail column "Liquid Kitchen" with Patterson's Beverage Journal (now The Tasting Panel), feature cover stories, contributing articles, and one online multimedia super feature story on Cognac with Sante Magazine, titled "The Sleeping Spirit". Aside form creating 60+ signature cocktails, his bar line Cocktail Art Productions has produced 18 titles including seven books, two DVD's, an audio CD Book, cocktail recipe cards, calendars, and postcards.

As a culinary artist, he started his cocktail photography series in 2007. His custom Zazzle store (zazzle.com/KBranche) uses 70 drink images from this series on a variety of everyday products and specialty items, including USPS-approved Cocktail Postage Stamps, Coffee Mugs, Greeting Cards, Men's and Women's T-Shirts and Hoodies, iPod Cases, iPad Cases, iPhone cases, Mousepads, Postcards, Hats, Aprons, Necklaces, Prints and Posters, all just for a fun and creative artistic outlet. Kyle also created and designed a board game called "Cocktail Hotel."

He's also co-produced and co-hosted the cocktail shows "Liquid Kitchen" and "Beverage Road," has written a treatment for a one-hour dramatic television series titled "Life Behind Bars," played the character of "Clive, the Bartender from the Dead" in the short film "The Hounds of Bakersfield," and the part of "Lyle the Bartender" in the upcoming feature film "Frozen Tundra." Other on-camera work includes his two Cocktail Art DVD's of "live and close-up" specialty and classic drink preparations.

Made in the USA
Charleston, SC
11 August 2015